THE ESSENTIAL GUIDE FOR THE SINGLE GUY

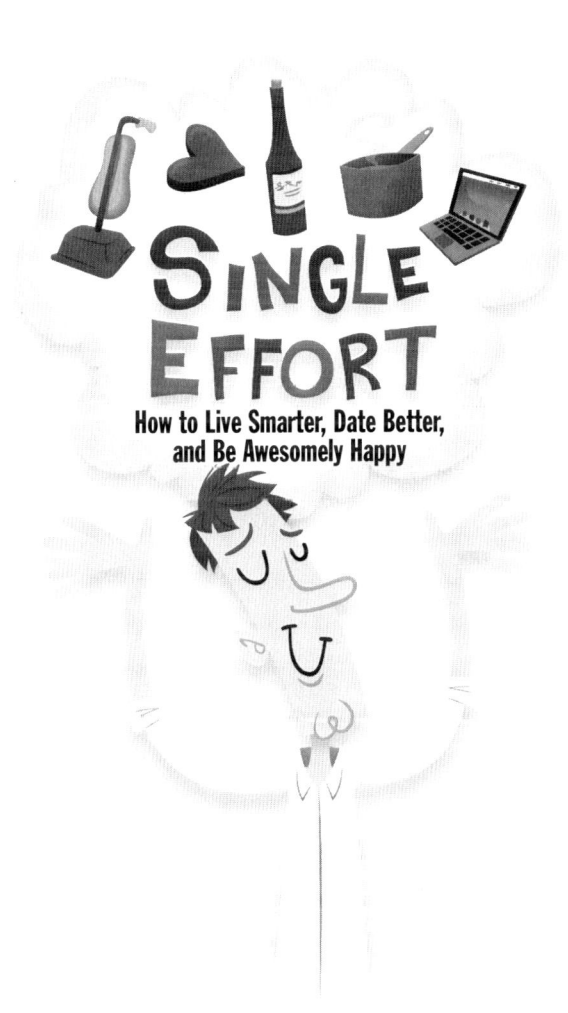

SINGLE EFFORT

How to Live Smarter, Date Better, and Be Awesomely Happy

JOE KELLER

scruffy olive

Copyright © 2013 by Joe Keller. All rights reserved.

No part of this publication may be reproduced, distributed, or transmitted in any form or by any means, or stored in a database or retrieval system, without the prior written permission of the publisher. Exceptions are made for brief excerpts used in published reviews.

Inquiries about this book should be addressed to the publisher:
Scruffy Olive, LLC
2960 Auburn Rd #214167
Auburn Hills, MI 48321-4167
(888) 562-9954 or info@scruffyolive.com
www.scruffyolive.com

While the publisher and author have used their best efforts in preparing this book, they make no representations or warranties with respect to the accuracy or completeness of the contents of this book and specifically disclaim any implied warranties of merchantability or fitness for a particular purpose. The advice and strategies contained herein may not be suitable for your situation. You should consult with a professional where appropriate.

Summary: Practical pointers and real-world advice for living a dynamic, happy, and successful life as a single guy.

Library of Congress Control Number: 2012916047

Paperback ISBN: 978-0-9849368-0-9
eBook ISBN: 978-0-9849368-1-6

Editor: Jean Borger at www.jeanborger.com
Book Design: Karrie Ross at www.karrieross.com
Cover illustration: André Jolicoeur at www.doodlemachine.com
Cover Text: Graham Van Dixhorn at www.writetoyourmarket.com;
    Jean Borger.
Index: Michael Bell at www.syndeticsystems.com

This book is available at quantity discounts for bulk purchases. For information please contact the publisher at (888) 562-9954 or info@scruffyolive.com.

Contents

Acknowledgments vii

Introduction: A Single Book…for Guys! 1
   Making It Meaningful for You 3
   Two Big Ideas for Single Guys 5
   Off You Go! 7

Chapter 1: Navigating Your Divorce 9
   Counseling Can Help 10
   Alternatives to Slugging It Out in Court 11
   Attorneys – Why You'll Still Need One 14
   Taking Stock of Your Stuff – His and Hers 15
   Kids First 17

Chapter 2: After the Breakup 19
   Avoiding the Rebound 20
   Creating a Bucket List 21
   Planning for a New Living Space 22
   Cutting Out the Clutter 25

Chapter 3: Outfitting Your New Living Space 29
   Enter the Internet 30
   A BBB Purchase Palooza 32
   Being Frugal, Single Effort Style 34
   Staying Safe (And Avoiding Used Underwear) 36
   A List to Get You Started 39
   A Smattering of Product Recommendations 40

Chapter 4: Creating a Female-Friendly Home 55
   A "Maid In" Voyage for Your Home 56
   The Inverse Cleaning Theory of Hotness 60
   A Slice of Pizza with That Dry Cleaning? 62

Field-Tested Cleaning Products That Work! 63
Some Do's and Don'ts 71
Your Plants and Flowers –
May They Live Long & Prosper................................76

Chapter 5: You're Cooking Now! 81
Getting Started 82
Meez Ahn Plahs, Please 83
A Basic Kitchen Setup, Minus the Plywood 86
Four Essential Ingredients 91
Salt and Pepper to Taste 101

Chapter 6: Top Single Effort Recipes 103
Sweet and Spicy BBQ Sauce 106
Fire-and-Forget Slow Cooker Chicken BBQ 108
Winner, Winner Creamy Chicken Dinner! 109
Wonderfully Fresh Chicken Caesar Salad 111
Zesty Short Ribs 114
Idahoan Mashed Potatoes
(The Easiest Side Dish Evah!).................................118
Easy Peasy Hard-Boiled Eggs....................................119
A Side of Toasted Baguette Slices 121
Mini Graham Cracker Jell-O Pudding Pie Dessert 123
Creamy Fruit Dip (Aka Foolproof Dessert).................125

Chapter 7: "Wining" for All the Right Reasons 127
Two Simple Facts About Wine...................................129
Red and White Demystified (When Purple = Red) 130
Six Types of Wine Reviewed 132
Where to Find Great Wine 140
Storing Your Wine for Maximum Flavor.....................140
Fare Thee Well, Wine. How Do I Serve Thee?............142
Pairing Your Wine with Food 143

Contents   v

Chapter 8: Meeting New Women – Stack the
    Odds in Your Favor!...147
  Where to Meet Women 148
  Where? Foraging for Food..149
  Where? Joining a Group Fitness Class........................150
  Where? Volunteering Your Time 151
  Where? Learning How to Dance.................................152
  Where? Joining an Organization.................................153
  Where? Enrolling in a Class..154
  Where? Shopping in a Women's Store 155
  Where? Some Parting Thoughts 156

Chapter 9: Approaching and Talking to Women (KISS)..157
  Mind Your Appearance...159
  Approach with Confidence...166
  Create an Interesting Dialogue...................................167
  Leave Her Wanting More..170
  So Long! So What? Move On. 172

Chapter 10: Before You Begin Dating… 175
  A Good Knight Revisited 176
  Your Dating Kit..179
  Who Pays for What?..183
  Some Additional Tips 186
  Establishing Ground Rules When Kids Are Involved ..188

Chapter 11: Your Two First Dates...................................191
  First Date #1 – The Mini-Date and Recommended
    Locations 192
  First Date #1 – Time for a First Kiss? (Her Body
    Language Holds the Key)..194
  First Date #1 – A Thank You Is in Order....................195
  First Date #1 – Keep Stepping Up to the Plate 198

First Date #2 – Your First Big Date and
   Recommended Locations..199
First Date #2 – Locations and Activities to Avoid 205
Creative Ideas to Keep the Relationship
   Magic Flowing..207
Using Technology to Maintain the Connection...........214
Revisiting Your Inner Compass....................................215

Chapter 12: Success with Online Dating.........................217
Sitting Idle at Step 2 – A Failed Dating Strategy..........218
Your Profile – Two Critical Elements 219
Profile Element #1 – Your Photos................................220
Profile Element #2 – Your Background.......................225
Recipe for a Compelling Background 230
A Sample Background 232
Capturing Her Attention with Your
   Introductory Email...234
A Sample Introductory Email 240

Chapter 13: Continuing Adventures in Online Dating....243
Your Personal Info (The Orange Peel Consideration)...244
Dating Multiple Women (Variety Is the Spice of Life)...246
Keeping Track of the Details..249
Thanks, But No Thanks…Revisited.............................250

Chapter 14: And Then, She Kissed Me............................253

Glossary 255
Index 263
About the Author 277

Acknowledgments

This book would not have been possible without the tremendous help and support of my close friends. Not only have they provided encouragement to complete this project, but they've been there with me through thick and thin, helping me through my divorce and easing my transition back into single life.

I owe a huge debt of gratitude to Bekah Eslin, David Naumowicz, Gerry Miller, Jeff Hampton, Ken Pasini, Kirt Manecke, and Marija Bulatovic – without whose friendship, guidance, and support I'd likely still be spinning in indecision, wondering what to do with the rest of my life.

Special thanks as well to Art, a very wise counselor who helped me focus on what is truly important in life, and to Barbara, a very skilled mediator who helped keep my divorce proceedings manageable and minimally painful.

Also, a thank you to Jeffrey Mar, whose wine expertise was invaluable (and tasty!).

I'd be severely remiss if I didn't also give giant kudos to my editor, Jean Borger, without whom this book would've been a jumbled mess.

Finally (and most importantly), I'm deeply grateful to my children, Nicholas and Kennedy, who are my inspiration, my hope, and the light of my life. I love you both very much!

Introduction

A Single Book...for Guys!

Before you read this book, you should know that I'm a regular guy – a guy who grew up middle class in the Midwest with my mother and two younger brothers. I'm not a counselor, therapist, psychologist, or any other professional in relationship theory, but after going through my divorce, I could probably play all those roles.

My story begins several years ago when I began to feel like something was missing in my marriage. This was a strange realization because my wife and I were relatively happy. We were living the American dream – great friends, a beautiful home, wonderful vacations, and material indulgences most guys would appreciate. From a beefy street motorcycle to a basement full of power tools, I had virtually every creature comfort I wanted.

My wife was a stay-at-home mom who took great care of our children, took pride in preparing home-cooked meals, volunteered on the PTO, and participated in many of the kids' school functions.

Sounds ideal, right? But, as may be typical for younger couples who become parents, my wife and I had let our marriage slip. We had focused more on being parents to our children and performing everyday household chores than we had on nurturing our own relationship. Divorce became the outcome when, after 13 years of marriage, we realized we had very few things remaining in common – we'd simply grown too far apart.

Embracing the reality of an unpleasant situation is always difficult. This was certainly the case for me when, at age 40, I faced the end of my marriage. When I started my own journey through divorce and back into single life, I couldn't find many quality guideposts to help me along the way. There are many books written on the subject of being single, some even focusing on the man's perspective, but none that tell it like it really is and give practical, real-world advice for single men.

Single Effort is intended to fill this gap – to provide practical advice from a regular guy who has experienced divorce and the transition back into bachelorhood and dating. I wrote it to provide support and encouragement (and a healthy dose of humor!) to all the single or soon-to-be-single guys out there who are straining to live life to its fullest.

This book is for you if you're facing a divorce or the end of a long-term relationship, or if you've already re-established yourself as a single guy after a breakup. This book will also be of interest to men *and* women who are still together and looking for ideas to spice up their relationship, and to women who are interested in a guy's perspective on relationships and dating (ladies, we're more than just beer and football – well, most of the time, anyway!).

Making It Meaningful for You

In these pages you'll find useful pointers on everything from acclimating to single life, to cooking a great meal, to finding the best places to meet and date new women. Each section stands on its own and may be referenced individually, so feel free to read straight through or skip around to find the sections that are most meaningful to you. You'll also find a handy glossary at the back of the book in case you come across a concept discussed previously and need a refresher.

Though the majority of the book assumes that you're already single, I've included a chapter on the big "D" to help those who find themselves currently embroiled in that difficult process. For those navigating a divorce, the challenges are many, and we discuss some important issues, such as the benefits of hiring a mediator, how to divide your property, and how to keep a strong focus on your kids (if you have kids). This chapter is designed to help you keep your priorities clear and minimize pain and frustration as you navigate the divorce process.

If you're already through your breakup or divorce (and don't really want to think about it anymore) feel free to skip ahead. The rest of the book is packed with practical advice meant just for you.

You'll discover that hiring a housekeeper can actually save you time and money – but hiring a "hot" one may create other problems – and you'll learn a sure-fire way to look your best whenever you leave home (leveraging the "Paparazzi Test"), among other indispensable skills. You'll also find that, more often than not, simple is better – such as what to say to a woman you've just met at a party or in a chance encounter at the grocery store.

Throughout the book (and on the Single Effort website at **www.SingleEffort.com**), you'll find straightforward recommendations that are simple to use and easy to remember. You can also use the website to send me your thoughts or questions, or email me directly at **heyjoe@SingleEffort.com**.

Look around and find what you need to create the life that's right for you!

Two Big Ideas for Single Guys

This book is full of useful pointers and tips that will improve your odds of living a happy and successful single life, but two stand out as particularly valuable. You'll encounter them throughout the book and on the Single Effort website.

1. **Single Effort (This idea is so important, I named the book after it!)**

The "Single Effort" Pointer

You know better than anyone – as a single guy, you're busy! As a father of two, I've learned to work smart, maximize my time, and multiply my outcomes. The expression "kill two birds with one stone" describes this effect but I like to express it differently – I call it "Single Effort."

An example of Single Effort would be keeping yourself in shape (or getting back in shape) while at the same time finding opportunities to meet new women by attending a group aerobics class. In my experience, aerobics classes are mostly filled with the opposite sex. So they offer an opportunity to meet new women while at the same time getting or keeping fit. And as your physique improves, so too will your comfort level and confidence with the women you meet. Improving your health, confidence, and dating prospects all in one fell swoop? Now *that's* Single Effort!

Single Effort isn't just about maximizing your time, though. It's also about making an effort – being proactive, charting your own course, and living a fulfilling life – in your single life and beyond!

Throughout the book, the Single Effort pointer will highlight opportunities for smart, but also bold, living.

2. The Good Knight (Because being a Good Knight can lead to a good night!)

The "Good Knight" Pointer

Single guys like to succeed with the ladies. A sure-fire way to do this is to adopt a "Good Knight" way of life and practice chivalry in all you do. "Chivalry" is a term born of the medieval institution of knighthood signifying gallantry, courtesy, and honor – the qualities of an ideal knight. Today, chivalry (also known as "doing what your mother taught you") still conveys consideration and respect for women.

Adopting a Good Knight way of life means practicing chivalry not just at parties or on dates when you want to impress a woman, but simply as a matter of course in your everyday life. For example, you may find yourself walking toward a door at work at the same time as a woman. Open the door for her and let her walk in first. Did the woman sitting next to you drop her napkin? Pick it up for her. Are you walking through a parking lot in the rain with your umbrella? Find a woman without one and offer to help keep her dry.

You'll find opportunities to be a Good Knight described throughout the book. When you see one, take note and try it out – you might be pleasantly surprised at the result!

Off You Go!

One last thing before you start your journey. To all the single (or soon-to-be-single) guys out there in search of help and advice, know that you are not alone – many guys have walked this path before you and faced the same challenges.

Since my divorce, I've learned a great deal about moving from the world of marriage into life as a single guy. My goal is to give you the benefit of learning from my successes and my many mistakes, and to help you take advantage of the collected experiences and wisdom of those who've gone before you.

Like many guys who have walked this path before, you too can emerge happier, healthier, and more successful by all measures. I wish you the best of luck on your journey!

CHAPTER 1

Navigating Your Divorce

Divorce is a big step for any guy. The decision to get a divorce – whether it's yours, your spouse's, or mutual – will likely be one of the most important decisions of your life. It may be more important than the decision to get married. With marriage comes the promise of happiness and prosperity. With divorce comes the very real prospect of lost income, loss of your home, and less time with your children (if you have children) – not to mention difficult emotions like sadness, anger, fear, and anxiety.

However, it's not all doom and gloom – far from it. Many times a divorce is just a stepping stone to a better life. Whether the decision to divorce was yours or not, there are undoubtedly things about your marriage you didn't like and things that your marriage prevented you from pursuing.

Though it can be difficult to see until after the dust has settled (sometimes *long* after the dust has settled), divorce can be liberating. It can give you the freedom to pursue life in the way you've always wanted, giving you a chance to follow new interests and passions, meet new and interesting people, and ultimately, find yourself in a happier place.

While it can be hard to see the positives of divorce while you're going through it, there are a number of things you can do to make the best of a tough situation and ensure the smoothest possible landing for yourself as you move into single life. Whether you chose divorce or divorce chose you, by leveraging the resources you have at your disposal you'll be able to set yourself up for success in both your work and your personal life. If you have kids, you'll also be able to ensure that they remain a top priority.

Counseling Can Help

To help sort things out and gain an objective perspective when my wife and I were contemplating divorce, we sought the advice of two professionals – the first, a marriage counselor we visited together for almost a year, and the second, an individual counselor I saw for six months.

Heading into counseling, I have to admit I had my doubts. Quite honestly, it's painful talking openly about emotional topics with a relative stranger. Doing so is in direct conflict with the "guy code," the one we all signed up for at birth. Most of us guys would rather bottle up our emotions, keep everything locked down tight, and avoid talking about our problems.

This certainly was the case for me. I dreaded the weekly pilgrimage to the counselor's office where I was often encouraged to express myself honestly, face my fears, and meet the situation head on. What I eventually discovered, however, was that telling someone else how you feel can be immensely therapeutic. While often difficult, the process can help you arrive at answers more quickly than if you were working through things alone. The ongoing dialogue helped me understand my feelings and in the end, I realized I'd become a stronger person for it.

It's also optimal to try to accommodate the needs of both parties when it comes to counseling. This means that you and your spouse might attend together even if just one of you is interested in counseling. Even when one party has strong doubts that a marriage can be saved, both parties will likely end up with more perspective and closure following joint counseling and this will definitely help ease some of the burdens of divorce after the fact (if divorce is the outcome).

I would also urge guys not to shy away from individual counseling. The time leading up to and following a divorce can be very challenging, and counseling, with a trained therapist or a trusted person of faith, can help you uncover underlying feelings and deal with them in a constructive way. In the end this will only help you – both in your new life as a single guy and when you decide to venture out into the dating world again.

Alternatives to Slugging It Out in Court

If you're moving full speed ahead down the path to divorce and contemplating slugging your case out in court, there are two alternatives to consider that could save you both money and emotional anguish: drafting your own divorce settlement and hiring a mediator.

Look at it this way – what's the worst that can happen if you attempt to draft your own settlement? You and your spouse might not agree and you may need to enlist the help of a mediator or take the matter to court. You probably would've done that anyway – so what's the harm in trying an alternative route first?

But if drafting your own settlement isn't possible – and it's not for most couples – the next best option may be to hire a mediator. The purpose of a mediator is to act as an unbiased intermediary, guiding you and your soon-to-be-ex through the divorce process in an effort to reach a settlement you can both live with.

You can think of a divorce mediator as a referee in a basketball game. An official that doesn't have a vested interest in either party and is present to keep things fair and call fouls when necessary. Both husband and wife must agree to participate, but once that hurdle is cleared, you'll have the advantage of actively determining the outcome of your divorce instead of leaving it up to attorneys and the court system to decide.

I've made some really bone-headed decisions in my life (like the time in high school when I decided to have a water fight in the house with my friends by dragging both garden hoses inside – that didn't turn out so well). But during my divorce I bucked the trend and made a really *good* decision. In fact, it was probably the best decision I made during that time. I decided, with my soon-to-be-ex's consent, to hire a mediator to arbitrate our divorce.

There are several benefits to hiring a mediator. For one, it changes what's normally a very adversarial process (one in which your attorney is doing his/her best to award your wife as little as possible and your wife's attorney is attempting to do the same to you) into a set of more productive conversations that the mediator guides and controls. Because the mediator is working in the best interest of both parties – not just one side – the tone and outcome can be much more positive.

Another benefit is that a mediated divorce will generally cost much less. In an adversarial divorce, much of the dialogue you send to your wife, and that she sends to you, will go through your attorneys, and attorneys charge for any use of their time, of course. In addition, in a mediated divorce, you're only paying for one person's time (the mediator) as opposed to two (your respective attorneys). In the end the costs associated with a mediated divorce can be less than half what you'd pay otherwise.

Finally, mediation can go a long way toward reducing the frustration and emotional pain of divorce. Spats or heated arguments with your soon-to-be-ex are less likely – the mediator generally quashes arguments quickly and helps keep discussions flowing in a positive direction.

During my divorce mediation my soon-to-be-ex and I were having difficulty agreeing on how much I should pay her for spousal support. She was asking for eight years of support – something I thought was unwarranted given only 13 years of marriage – and I was asking for only three years. We both argued our points in front of our mediator and were becoming very frustrated by the other's unwillingness to budge.

When the atmosphere in the room turned heated, our mediator intervened – proposing more years of spousal support than I was offering but at the same time asking my soon-to-be-ex to purchase her own medical insurance and to also receive a smaller percentage of my bonuses.

In the end, we both begrudgingly agreed to the mediator's terms (as the saying goes, the sign of a good compromise is that no one gets exactly what they want). Contrast this with us trying to come to the same agreement solely through attorneys. Our emotions would likely have gotten the better of us, causing heated discussions that would've dragged on for weeks, only adding to the frustration and emotional pain we were both feeling (not to mention the cost).

Before you rush out to hire a mediator, however, first consider whether one is even needed. You may be getting along well enough with your soon-to-be-ex to draft your own divorce settlement as previously discussed (which will mean even more cost savings and less heartache for you). Alternatively, if your situation doesn't allow you to hire a mediator or draft your own settlement, you'll have no choice but to hitch your divorce buggy to your attorneys.

Attorneys – Why You'll Still Need One

Even if you have the luxury of drafting your own divorce decree or working with a mediator, there will still be a need to involve attorneys in your divorce process (most likely, one for you and one for your spouse). An attorney will help you understand the implications of legal terms used in the divorce decree that you may not be familiar with. Terms like *legal custody*, *custodial parent*, *garnishment*, *physical custody*, and *community property* all have important implications in the eyes of the law.

In addition, an attorney will review any child support or alimony being offered to ensure it's within the boundaries of what your state considers fair and equitable (given the financial circumstances of both parties). Most states have well-worn formulas in place that recommend what, if anything, you should be paying for child support and alimony. Your attorney can run the numbers based on your set of circumstances.

And finally, once your settlement is near completion, you'll want an attorney to review the entire document from your perspective to confirm you're getting a fair deal – before you endorse anything with your signature.

In either case, however – whether you've drafted the divorce decree on your own or have hired a mediator – keep your attorney on a short leash. Make sure they know up front, before you hire them, that you don't want them to "stir the pot" and undo all that you've agreed to. Emphasize that you're asking them to review the draft agreement to ensure you're getting a fair deal and that there aren't any glaring mistakes or omissions.

Hopefully, you and your ex won't have to spend more than $2,000 in attorney fees to review your draft divorce decree ($1,000 for your attorney and $1,000 for hers). And if you've gone down the mediation path, most likely your mediator will have a list of attorneys they've already used and can recommend to you.

According to an article on About.com, the average cost of a divorce in the United States is $15,000 ("How Much Will My Divorce Cost?" by Cathy Meyer, www.divorcesupport.about.com/od/financialissues/f/costofdivorce.htm). From start to finish, including the mediator, my attorney to review the divorce decree, my ex's attorney to review the divorce decree, all legally prepared documents, and finally, court fees, the total for my divorce was $6,000 (less than half the average cost).

Although $6,000 is still a lot of money, it shows that it is indeed possible to limit divorce costs. The whole process would've been much more expensive (and more heated) had we not used a mediator and instead fought it out in court.

Taking Stock of Your Stuff – His and Hers

Regardless of how you go through your divorce – on your own, mediated, or adversarial – you'll need to divide up everything you own with your soon-to-be-ex. This includes trivial ownership, like who gets the bathroom scale, to more important use rights, like who takes possession of the heirloom china.

Documenting who gets what early on will save you heartache later, nipping arguments in the bud when disagreements flare up over ownership. Your best bet is to try to get through this process without the costly addition of lawyers. To this end, set aside some time to work through ownership issues one on one with your spouse.

If possible, spend half a day walking through your home with your soon-to-be-ex documenting each and every item you own – large and small – no matter how insignificant it may seem at the time.

During this walkthrough, carry a clipboard with several sheets of paper that will act as your inventory worksheet. Divide each sheet of paper into four columns – one column for the item name (e.g. silverware, microwave, grandfather clock, etc.) and three check mark columns labeled "His," "Hers," and "Unresolved."

An inventory worksheet for dividing up material possessions between you and your spouse

Write down each item you encounter in a separate row under the "Item" heading and then put a check mark in either the "His" or "Hers" column based on what you both agree. If there's a disagreement about who should get a particular item, don't try to solve it then and there. Instead, place a check mark in the "Unresolved" column and move on to the next item. You can revisit the "Unresolved" column after a few days have passed – giving both of you time to reflect on which items you truly want. When you've finished the worksheet, initial it with your spouse and make a copy for each of you.

> For help dividing up and keeping track of your possessions, you can download an inventory worksheet (like the one on the previous page) at **www.SingleEffort.com/free**.

Finally, once you and your spouse have divided up your belongings, start developing a new list just for yourself. This list should contain everything you need to acquire before you begin living on your own. If you can, start planning well in advance of your move – at least three months, if you can swing it. Take this time to reach out to friends who may have extra household items they no longer need and to research any purchases you plan to make to ensure you're getting the right product for your needs and the best value for your money (for more on outfitting your new home, including frugal options, see chapter 3).

Kids First

If there are kids involved as you enter into the divorce process, do your best to always give them top priority. If you find yourself in disagreements with your soon-to-be-ex and are not sure what direction to follow, consider the well-worn litmus test, "Is this in the best interest of my kids?"

During my divorce the soon-to-be-ex and I (thankfully) were able to divide up most of our household items without issue. The lone exception was an antique set of pink glass mixing bowls that had been given to us by my grandmother. My grandmother had used the bowls her entire adult life and had passed them on to us as an heirloom for safekeeping.

The bowls were still in very good shape and held sentimental value for me, but my soon-to-be-ex insisted they should go with her. As much as I wanted the bowls, I decided to let her have them so the kids wouldn't see us arguing about something that, to them, would've looked pretty ridiculous (grown adults arguing over a set of pink mixing bowls).

In the end, regardless of whether you or your spouse chose divorce and whatever your viewpoint on it, life *is* going to change for your children. However, divorce by itself doesn't doom them to years of emotional problems or a lifetime of anxiety. Rather, it's their exposure to parental conflict and unhealthy situations both during and after the divorce that will have the greatest impact on their life.

Do your best to keep your children out of the middle of your divorce proceedings and stay focused on their well-being. Take time to listen to their thoughts. Continue to love them unconditionally. Give them all that you can, and rest a bit easier knowing they'll be just fine.

CHAPTER 2

After the Breakup

From my marriage and divorce I learned an important lesson – one I wish I'd been smart enough to understand years ago. I learned that happiness is *the* key to living a good life. And quite frankly, if we boil it all down – if we take away all the day-to-day issues we encounter at home and at work, if we sit down and ponder it – what we're really looking for is simply to be happy.

Through the upheaval of my divorce, I came to realize that true happiness cannot come from anything external – it must resonate from within. And I found myself wondering what happiness meant to me. After a good deal of thought, I arrived at this definition: "Happiness is knowing who you are and being at peace with yourself."

Without getting too abstract (this is a practical book, after all) I encourage you to develop your own definition of happiness and then keep that definition in mind as you move through your single life. This definition can be your compass, helping you stay on the right path to finding what you seek, both in life and in love.

With your internal compass pointing to what you desire as you work through the challenging – but also liberating – time after your breakup, you'll find yourself more confident, more outgoing, and much more likely to find the happiness you seek.

Avoiding the Rebound

Inner happiness is the key not only to living a fruitful life, but also to finding the right partner. Indeed, you need to learn to be happy on your own first so you don't *need* a partner but instead *want* a partner – an important distinction.

Unfortunately, after a breakup, many men (and women, for that matter) will jump right back into a new relationship. You've probably heard about, and maybe even experienced, the lessons learned from "dating on the rebound" – where a guy starts dating immediately after a divorce or the end of a long-term relationship.

There are many reasons we, as guys, go down this path. One of the most common is that it helps distract us from the pain we're experiencing with our breakup. A rebound relationship offers comfort and emotional support, along with companionship. Although rebound dating fills your time with a new relationship, it also has an unfortunate consequence – it diverts focus away from finding what it is you're looking for, both in your life and, if desired, in a life partner.

After the end of a marriage or long-term relationship, allow yourself time to explore being "you" before you begin dating. Consider rekindling old friendships or taking up a new hobby that you've always wanted to pursue – or simply spend time reflecting on what you want to do with the next chapter in your life.

Maybe you've always wanted to run with the bulls in Spain, learn how to snowboard in Colorado, spend time alone in the wilderness, solve a Rubik's Cube, or learn to play the guitar. The point is to take some down time, to seize the opportunity in between relationships to rediscover what makes you truly happy.

There's a balance that needs to be embraced in any newly single life. A focus on your children, if you have any, is important. But equally important is making sure you take the time to discover and follow your own interests and passions. So take time to simply be yourself and to discover your true inner happiness – before you begin dating and meeting new people.

Creating a Bucket List

After your breakup is final and you've been on your own for a bit, you may start to ponder what you'd still like to accomplish in your life. No doubt your "to-do" list will be fairly long – we all have big dreams and aspirations! One way to motivate yourself to achieve your lifelong goals is to create a "bucket list."

The concept of a bucket list has been around for some time but it received a boost in 2007 from the movie of the same name. The film's two main characters, Carter Chambers (Morgan Freeman) and Edward Cole (Jack Nicholson), meet in a hospital after both being diagnosed with a terminal illness. They become friends and create a bucket list – the things they want to do before they "kick the bucket" – and the movie chronicles their often humorous adventures working to accomplish everything on their list.

My bucket list currently stands at over 30 entries and contains a wide range of aspirations. Things on my list include taking a tour of the U.S. by RV camper, owning a European sports car, writing two books (one for grown-ups and one for kids – put a check mark in one of those columns!), bungee jumping off a tall bridge, visiting ten foreign countries (and no, Canada and Mexico don't count – although they're fine places to visit), starting a nonprofit organization, and sending both kids through college.

If you decide to create a bucket list, consider committing it to paper and then placing the list in a location where you can view it weekly, if not daily. Documenting your goals helps solidify them, taking them from the realm of "wishful thinking" into the realm of "this is what I've set for myself to accomplish." It provides a constant reminder of what you want to achieve.

As simple as it sounds, writing down what you want to accomplish in life, your bucket list, will not only help you achieve your goals, it'll give you the opportunity to reflect on what you want out of life, *before* you invest in new relationships.

> To get a jump-start on creating your own bucket list visit **www.bucketlist.org** – they have thousands of fantastic ideas. Use them as thought-starters for planning, then achieving, your own dreams and ambitions!

Planning for a New Living Space

Just like taking time to review your lifelong goals, if you're moving into a new living space after a breakup (or you're staying but she's moving out of your space), set aside some time to plan.

For those coming off a divorce who are looking for a new place to live, consider renting an apartment for the first year.

After a divorce you'll need to focus your time and energy on establishing a new life for yourself and your children (if children are involved) – not on worrying about cutting the lawn, shoveling snow, fixing a leaky faucet, repairing the furnace, or sealing a drafty window.

With a rental, you can leave the maintenance headaches to the property owner and focus instead on getting your new single life in order. Then if you miss the home ownership experience, you can always purchase a new home after the first year is over.

Once you've identified where you're going to live, take time to review your space requirements. Consider developing a floor plan for each major room, and do this prior to settling in (or settling back in if she's moving out). This will help you to both maximize your available space and ensure that it looks thoughtfully arranged – something that women will appreciate and admire when they visit (chapter 4 discusses why it's important that your home be female friendly – and provides suggestions for how to make it more so).

Set aside time to measure each room's dimensions and record the measurements on paper. In addition, record rough measurements for all your large household items (e.g. living room couch, beds, bedroom dressers, kitchen table, widescreen TV, etc.).

When you have some quiet time to yourself, take out a couple sheets of graph paper and transfer the measurements of each room to the graph paper in scale (a common scale is one square on the graph paper equals one foot in the real world). Once the rooms have been placed in proper scale on the graph paper you can then thoughtfully lay out where the furniture will go.

When I found an apartment after my divorce, I realized planning for this move was going to be different from my previous moves when I was married. This time, I was going to be taking all the measurements for the floor plan by myself.

Because a tape measure is a bit unwieldy to use alone to record long measurements, I invested in a small ultrasonic measuring tool. An ultrasonic measuring tool is ideal for use by someone working alone. It uses sonic waves to calculate distances with just the touch of a button (you can find these handy tools at most do-it-yourself retailers for under $40).

With the ultrasonic measuring tool, I was done measuring in under 20 minutes – and I had a useful new tool to add to my collection!

> If you have children, Single Effort the development of your floor plan by involving your kids. You'll enjoy the benefit of getting a different perspective on how to set up the living space and they'll appreciate having a say in where things are going to go in their new home.

Also, if children are involved and you're moving, make sure you place some of their favorite things from their old home in your new living space. This could be as simple as a couple of family pictures or several of their prized stuffed animals, to as involved as large pieces of bedroom furniture. Having familiar things in your new home will help your children feel safe and ease them into their new surroundings.

On this same point, take pains to ignore the temptation to rid yourself of everything from your past life. For example, if your children want to hang a picture of their mom in their room, let them (just not in your main living area – chapter 4 touches on why). Even if you don't want to be reminded of your ex, your children still do. It's their mom and they need to keep the connection back to her.

And one last point if children are involved and you're moving to a new location – prior to your move don't forget to send updated contact information to their school. This is easy to overlook until you miss an important mailing. It's also beneficial to instruct your children's school to mail out two copies of their report cards – one to you and one to their mother – so you're both always on top of their grades (this is less important as everything goes digital, but many schools still deliver report cards the old-fashioned way).

Cutting Out the Clutter

After a breakup – when moving into a new home or refurnishing an existing space – consider seizing the opportunity to hit the big, red "reset" button on your inventory of possessions. This is an ideal time to cut out the needless clutter that's been accumulating over the years and to focus on what's important in your life.

After I found my apartment and began to develop a floor plan, I realized I was going to have to downsize my lifestyle quite a bit. Initially I was dismayed by the thought of going from a 2,800 square foot home to a 1,400 square foot apartment with two kids – but after just a few weeks in the apartment, I grew to love it.

Downsizing forced me to cut out the needless clutter I'd accumulated during my marriage. Because I was moving into a much smaller living space that I would share with my kids, I could only keep about 20% of what I owned – the rest would have to be sold, given to friends, or donated to charity.

Ridding myself of the many belongings I'd built up over 13 years of marriage, things I thought I "had to have," was actually very liberating. Did I really need to own enough power tools to fill an entire aisle at Home Depot? Doubtful. Was it really necessary to own a pressure washer strong enough to punch a hole in a 2x4 at a distance of 20 paces? Probably not (it was a lot of fun, though!).

Looking back on my marriage, I now realize I was constantly compensating for my unhappiness. One of the ways I did this was by buying things I rationalized I needed, but whose purchase in the end couldn't really be justified.

While working on cutting out my own clutter, I came across a poster at a local sandwich shop that hit home. Titled "How Much Is Enough?" (based on an original story by Heinrich Böll), it reinforced the lesson I was already learning – that less is sometimes more:

> *An American businessman was at the pier of a small Mexican coastal village when a small boat with just one fisherman docked. Inside the small boat were several large yellow-fin tuna. The American complimented the Mexican on the quality of his fish and asked how long it took to catch them. The Mexican replied only a little while. The American then asked why didn't he stay out longer and catch more fish. The Mexican said he had enough to support his family's immediate needs. The American then asked, but what do you do with the rest of your time? The Mexican fisherman said, "I sleep late, fish a little, play with my children, take siesta with my wife, Maria, and stroll into the village each evening where I sip wine and play guitar with my amigos – I have a full and busy life, señor."*
>
> *The American scoffed, "I am a Harvard MBA and could help you. You should spend more time fishing and with the proceeds buy a bigger boat, and with the proceeds*

from the bigger boat you could buy several boats – eventually you would have a fleet of fishing boats. Instead of selling your catch to a middleman, you would sell directly to the processor, eventually opening your own cannery. You would control the product, processing, and distribution. You would need to leave this small coastal fishing village and move to Mexico City, then L.A., and eventually New York City, where you would run your expanding enterprise." The Mexican fisherman asked, "But señor, how long will this all take?" To which the American replied, "15-20 years." "But what then, señor?"

The American laughed and said that's the best part. When the time is right you would announce an IPO and sell your company stock to the public and become very rich, you would make millions. "Millions, señor? Then what?" The American said, "Then you would retire and move to a small coastal fishing village where you would sleep late, fish a little, play with your kids, take siesta with your wife, and stroll to the village in the evenings where you could sip wine and play your guitar with your amigos."

If you're moving into a new lifestyle as a single guy, consider taking this opportunity to rid yourself of the clutter you no longer need. As the late, great comedian George Carlin once said, "Just cause you got the monkey off your back doesn't mean the circus has left town."

A relationship breakup may free you from the proverbial monkey but you'll still need to jettison the unnecessary clutter in your life – literally and figuratively – to ensure that the circus has left town. Doing so might mean living less "large," but you'll likely be much happier as a result!

CHAPTER 3

Outfitting Your New Living Space

When you begin living on your own, you may be surprised at the number of things you need to have on hand to maintain a base level of functionality – from kitchen sink mats and vacuum cleaners to hampers and hand towels. Whatever you don't have, you'll obviously need to acquire.

I started planning my move into my new apartment several months before my actual move-out-of-the-marital-home date. My ex was getting the majority of our household items, from silverware, to pots and pans, to even our clothes hangers. As a result, the list of what I needed was daunting – it included over 50 items!

In the past, this would've meant driving to dozens of stores and poking around the interior of various retail establishments. But there's a problem with this approach: if you shop the "old-fashioned" way by visiting a store and perusing the aisles to find what you need, how do you know what you're buying is the best product and value for your money? How do you know the vacuum cleaner you're standing in front of at your local

Sears store does a good job? Maybe the model sitting right next to it is better? Maybe there's one at the Best Buy down the road that does an even better job?

Without additional information you simply don't know. You rely on the salesperson (if you can find one), ads and commercials, or quite simply, what's printed on the product's packaging. When making a purchasing decision based on ads or packaging you are, in effect, relying on the manufacturer (whose job it is to make sure you buy their product regardless of how well it performs) for your information.

When you find yourself standing in front of a product in a store aisle, you don't have the benefit of a key piece of information – how the product actually performs in the real world. In order to make a sound purchasing decision, what you really need are reviews of the product's performance from everyday people who've already used it.

Enter the Internet

Enter the Internet. The Internet has been described as the Great Equalizer, elevating consumers by placing them on a level playing field with large, multinational corporations, and giving individuals an unprecedented ability to make purchasing decisions based on how well a product actually performs – not on how well it's packaged or marketed.

As someone who might be staring at a long list of items to buy for his home (and if you're currently in or have recently gone through the divorce process – most likely needing to preserve cash), you'll want to stretch your dollars as far as they'll go. Purchasing based on how well a product performs in the real world is the only way to ensure you get the most bang for your buck.

As I stared at the long list of items I needed for my apartment, I took this lesson to heart. I decided to leverage the Internet and purchase the majority of what I needed on Amazon.com (**www.amazon.com**).

Why Amazon? Three key reasons:

- Large selection of products
- Good prices
- (And most importantly) Informative product reviews

With almost every product Amazon offers for purchase you'll find real-life reviews by consumers who've used it. You'll find these reviews incredibly valuable in helping you decide which are the best products to use in your home.

Among the laundry list of items I needed to buy for my apartment was a vacuum cleaner (the first thing I wound up purchasing for my new home as a single guy). My previous vacuum cleaner was staying with my ex and I, frankly, didn't know a good vacuum from a bad vacuum. In this case, I was looking for something that did indeed "suck," but in a good, "clean your whole house" sort of way.

After only 30 minutes on Amazon I found the vacuum I wanted. It had an average of 4.5 stars out of 5 with over 500 customer reviews. When the vacuum arrived I put it through its paces and its performance was superb! The only thing that could've improved the experience would've been the addition of a cushy seat, cup holder, and self-propelled option so I could ride it around the apartment.

Even my housekeeper has exclaimed the virtues of this vacuum, and that says a lot – she's very particular when it comes to cleaning products and appliances (if the word "housekeeper" sounds outlandish to you at this point, don't object to it yet – in the next chapter you'll learn why it might make sense to hire a housekeeper and how it could actually end up *saving* you money).

If you decide to use Amazon for the first time (or you're already an Amazon convert) and you plan on buying more than a few items over the course of a year, consider purchasing an "Amazon Prime" membership. An Amazon Prime membership costs $79 a year (at the time of this book's publishing), but in return, gives you free two-day shipping on all items that Amazon stocks (some items Amazon sells are not stocked by Amazon but sold through third parties, so the shipping discount does not apply there).

My Prime membership has paid for itself several times over. I estimate I saved over $200 in shipping costs in just my first year of singleness. Since then I've renewed my membership every year, and it's proven its worth again and again.

Whether you're in the market for a new vacuum cleaner or any other household appliance, consider ditching the traditional brick and mortar and instead, leveraging the power of the Great Equalizer.

A BBB Purchase Palooza

Although online shopping can save you both time and money, there are some products you should steer clear of purchasing online without first experiencing them in person. These are products that you need to touch and feel – and see up close – before you buy. Examples would be items for your bath or bedroom like towels, bed sheets, pillows, and the like.

For household items you need to touch and feel, consider visiting a retail home goods store. One popular store that's very single-guy friendly is Bed Bath & Beyond. They carry a wide variety of household products and have a very unique and liberal coupon acceptance policy – the Bed Bath & Beyond (BBB) coupon policy allows most BBB stores to happily accept expired BBB coupons.

Of course, other retail stores will, from time to time, also accept expired coupons, but for BBB this policy is simply a matter of course. Because their coupons never expire you can stock up on them without ever having to worry about rushing to the store before they lose their value. I've used BBB coupons that were well over a year old without any problem at several BBB stores.

What makes this coupon acceptance policy even better is that many BBB coupons are quite valuable – some worth up to 20% off an individual item. I once had eight 20% off coupons (all well expired) that I used at the same time to buy eight items for my home and all were gladly accepted.

Can't find any BBB coupons in your local paper or coupon mailer? I was in the same boat so I decided to try eBay (**www.ebay.com**) and hit upon the mother lode. I bought a group of ten BBB 20% off coupons for $18 and with those coupons, saved over $90 on a BBB purchase palooza (a net savings of $72).

Simply visit eBay and search for "bed bath beyond coupons." (To be on the safe side, check with the BBB stores in your area to make sure they accept expired coupons before bidding.)

If you plan on regular excursions to BBB it may be wise to sign up for BBB's coupon mailer (you can sign up online or in-store). Once signed up you'll receive regular flyers and BBB coupons in the mail, which should help keep your coupon inventory full.

If you find you have extra BBB coupons, you can Single Effort your BBB shopping with meeting new women, and practice your Good Knight skills, all in one fell swoop! If you spot a woman in a BBB store that you'd like to meet, simply approach her with coupon in hand and explain that you have an extra you'd like to give her.

This is not only a great ice breaker but it's also a very chivalrous act. She should be sufficiently smitten by your generosity to allow for a conversation where you can get to know her and hopefully, come away with plans for a future date (if you feel a bit intimidated by the thought of striking up a conversation with a woman you don't know, fear not – chapter 9 has tips and recommendations to help you land the perfect conversation!).

Being Frugal, Single Effort Style

Acquiring household items for your new living space can be a big drain on your finances – even more so if you're going through a divorce and cash is in short supply. If you don't have ample financial resources available to buy new items for your home (or you're simply a thrifty shopper) consider the option of shopping at a resale store, visiting garage or yard sales, or hitting online sites like eBay or craigslist (**www.craigslist.org**).

There's no shame whatsoever in buying used items at a garage sale, resale shop, or online. I still shop at garage sales myself, mainly influenced by my mother early on. My mom started taking me with her to garage sales when I was very young (as she was always the frugal shopper) and we came away with some great finds.

I vividly remember one of the best garage sale purchases I ever made as a young boy: a large box of vintage GI Joe action figures complete with all their accompanying outfits and vehicles. It was a boy's dream come true! Looking back from a single-guy perspective, it's probably a good thing I didn't keep that collection. If I had, no doubt many of the action figures would still be prominently displayed in my apartment – thereby killing any hopes of a second date after a woman's first visit!

As you shop for your own rare finds, keep in mind that just like shopping in a BBB store, garage and yard sales can be fertile ground for meeting new women – and they're full of great ice breakers. If you see a woman you'd like to meet, Single Effort your garage sale shopping by selecting something you think she might be interested in, like an attractive vase, a popular novel, or unique jewelry. Then simply walk over to her with the item in hand and ask her opinion.

For example, walk over with an interesting necklace and ask if she thinks it's something a young girl would like (it could be a gift for your daughter or a niece), or pick up a novel by a popular author and ask her if she's read it. Use the item you're holding to get the conversation started and go from there. And if there's interest, consider setting up a Mini-Date to get to know her more (Mini-Dates are discussed in depth in chapter 11)!

Staying Safe (And Avoiding Used Underwear)

When acquiring products for your home, don't forget about home safety. Although you can find many items at yard sales and resale shops, there are some you should never consider buying used. Things like underwear, a toothbrush, beer, and pizza would probably be at or near the top of the list for most single guys.

But smart single guys will also want to add three essential home safety items to their list:
- Smoke detectors
- Carbon monoxide (CO) detectors
- Fire extinguishers

These three products are essential to any living space – if you don't own them already, consider purchasing and installing them in your home. However, the performance of each degrades overtime, so never buy then used. Here are a few facts and figures to help convince you to own at least one of each of the above.

Smoke and CO Detectors

According to the National Fire Protection Association, approximately 33% of American homes are not adequately protected with smoke detectors even though the death rate from fire is 45% lower when one working smoke detector is present. Underwriters Laboratories reports that two-thirds of residential fire deaths occurred in homes with no working alarms.

In addition, according to the *Journal of the American Medical Association*, there are approximately 2,100 unintentional deaths from CO every year. The use of CO detectors could prevent many of these fatalities.

Consumer Reports (www.consumerreports.org) regularly publishes reviews on smoke and CO detectors. For these items, don't skimp on price – purchase quality detectors, preferably one of each for each floor of your home. After installing smoke and CO detectors in your home, be sure to contact your insurance company. Many insurers will offer discounts for homes that have them.

Fire Extinguishers

The third essential item for any home is a fire extinguisher. If a fire starts in your home and you catch it in time, you can dramatically reduce property loss and save lives.

Fire extinguishers designed for home use are rated for their effectiveness on three classes of fires. Class "A" ratings are for combustibles such as wood, paper, and cloth. Class "B" ratings are for flammable liquids such as kerosene, oil, and gasoline. And the Class "C" designation means that the extinguisher can be used for electrical fires involving things like appliances or wiring.

Every extinguisher is rated for its effectiveness in two of the three categories, A and B. The numeric rating for these categories goes from 1 to 60 and appears in front of the letter – the higher the number the better.

For example, an extinguisher rated as "2-A" can put out approximately twice as much combustible fire as a "1-A" extinguisher. But an extinguisher rated as "4-B" can only put out half as much flammable-liquid fire as an "8-B" fire extinguisher. Extinguishers that can be used on electrical fires will also carry the letter "C," but numeric ratings are not used for the "C" category. Clear as mud, right? Not to worry – simply look for an extinguisher with a rating of "1-A, 10-B:C" (or higher). This is a typical rating for many household extinguishers.

Make sure the fire extinguisher you purchase is rated not only in the A and B categories (remember, the higher the number the better) but also carries the C designation for fighting electrical fires. You can find unbiased fire extinguisher reviews on Amazon.com and the Consumer Reports website.

In addition to placing at least one fire extinguisher in your home, consider placing a fire extinguisher in the trunk of your vehicle as well. Hopefully it'll never be needed but if it is, you'll be glad to have it handy!

During my first year of single life, a fog light that had worked itself free of its housing fell into the plastic front bumper casing of my car, burning a hole in the bumper and igniting the material around it. Luckily, this occurred while I was dropping my daughter off at her bus stop and the bus had just rolled up. I grabbed the extinguisher from the bus and put out the small fire (which showed no signs of stopping).

The situation could've gone from bad to worse quickly had the bus not pulled up when it did. I learned an important lesson that day – the unexpected is never expected – and now carry an extinguisher in my vehicle's trunk.

My vehicle's electrical fire – happily caught in time with the help of a nearby fire extinguisher!

(© Single Effort. Image courtesy of the author.)

Home safety should be a top priority when you move into your new living space. Once you've outfitted your space and your vehicle with the proper tools, relax a bit knowing that the risk of a situation going from bad to worse is greatly reduced. That is, unless you insist on eating day-old pizza in someone else's underwear – there's likely little help for you there!

A List to Get You Started

When striking out on your own, you'll have enough on your mind. It'll be easy to forget some of the many things you'll need to pick up for your home. To help you stay on track, a partial list of household items for single guys is provided here.

You may not require all the items listed below or you may need everything and more. A key point, however, is to create a list and work through it, researching the best value for your money on each item, hopefully well before you're living on your own.

> The complete list of 51 recommended items for your home is posted on the Single Effort website at **www.SingleEffort.com/free**. You can use it as a starting point for your own list. If you already have a list, you can compare the two to make sure you're not forgetting anything important.

Recommended items include:
- Baking sheets and pans
- Bedding, linens, pillows, and blankets
- Children's thermometer *
- Cocktail set
- Cups and glasses *

- Dining room table place mats
- Dinnerware set
- Dish drying rack
- Drink coasters
- Electric handheld mixer
- Emergency kit (band-aids, gauze, antibiotic, etc.)
- Food storage containers *
- Hand and bath towels for the bathroom
- Hand towels for the kitchen
- Kitchen and bathroom cleaning supplies
- Kitchen and bathroom soap dispensers *
- Kitchen knives *
- Kitchen sink mat
- Laundry hampers for each bedroom
- Liner for kitchen drawers
- Measuring cups
- Microwave splatter guard
- Mixing bowls
- Shoe trees *
- Vacuum
- Welcome mat
- Wine rack

* These items are reviewed in the next section.

A Smattering of Product Recommendations

To help you save time and money (and a bit of heartache) in selecting quality products for your home, several of the items contained in the preceding list are reviewed in this section.

Please note that no compensation is accepted from any company whose product is discussed or recommended here or listed on the website.

Most of the following products were purchased on Amazon.com and all are Single Effort tested and approved!

Glasses

I get tired of cups and glasses that constantly "sweat," leaving rings of moisture on tables and counters. I'm also weary of cups made of glass – they're not very kid friendly and they don't stand up to being dropped or bumped. On a recommendation from a girl+friend, I purchased a set of Tervis Tumblers, in both 16-ounce and 24-ounce sizes, and I couldn't be happier with how they perform!

Tervis Tumblers

(© Tervis at *www.tervis.com*)

> I use the term "girl+friend" when someone is a girl plus a good friend, but there is no romantic relationship involved. When romance *is* involved, I use "girlfriend." A slight difference in spelling but a huge difference in meaning!

Tervis Tumblers are made of a clear polycarbonate and are dishwasher, microwave, and freezer safe. They work their magic by utilizing a double-walled insulation design. They keep hot beverages hot longer and cold beverages cold longer – all without any condensation forming on the outside of the tumbler.

    Tervis Tumblers are very sturdy and have been dropped by my kids (and me) on many occasions without damage. And you know you've found a quality product when the manufacturer gives you a lifetime warranty on each one. The only downside is that these tumblers are a bit pricey. I consider Tervis Tumblers a great investment, though – it should be a long time before you have to buy another set of drinking glasses!

Shoe Tree

As the old saying goes, "Shoes make the man." One of the fundamental things a woman looks for in a well-dressed man is his shoes (recommendations on what to wear and what not to wear – including shoes *and* clothing – follow a bit later in chapter 9). The quality of your shoes and how well you take care of them will reveal a lot about you to the women you meet.

Woodlore Cedar Shoe Trees

(© Woodlore at **www.woodlore.com**)

For your leather shoes, I recommend doing what my father taught me – placing a shoe tree inside them when they're not being worn.

The benefits of using a shoe tree are many. Shoe trees:

- Help break in new shoes
- Keep the shape of shoes intact
- Absorb moisture that collects in the lining of shoes
- Smooth out any creases that develop in shoes after being worn

And possibly the most important benefit? *Cedar* shoe trees (the ones I recommend) also assist in the removal of foot odor – *not* something you want wafting about you as a newly single guy trying to make a good impression on women!

I've tried several shoe trees and found that Woodlore Cedar Shoe Trees work best. Woodlore uses real cedar in their products and they have an adjustable design that allows them to fit into a variety of shoe sizes. Many Woodlore trees (they sell several styles) also have a handy brass knob installed at the rear to make it easy to pull the tree from the shoe.

You can find less expensive shoe trees but they often aren't as nicely made. Due to their exceptional quality, I find Woodlore Cedar Shoe Trees to be the best value on the market!

Thermometer

For those with children, you know the drill. When a child is complaining about not feeling well it's helpful to take their temperature – to gauge if it's something minor like a tummy ache or something more serious like an infection. Many times a child's temperature is the deciding factor for whether or not you need to visit the doctor. I've struggled with a variety of thermometers. Old-fashioned mercury thermometers take too long to get a reading and many of the digital thermometers on the market are not accurate.

BD Rapid Flex Digital Thermometer

(Courtesy and © Becton, Dickinson and Company at **www.bd.com**. Reprinted with permission.)

On a recommendation from a doctor, I purchased the BD Rapid Flex Digital Thermometer and was pleasantly surprised by its speed and accuracy. The tip of the BD thermometer is inserted under the tongue and within a few seconds you have an accurate temperature measurement. If you have small children who won't sit still long enough to have their temperature taken with a mercury thermometer, you'll really appreciate the speed of the BD digital thermometer.

A thermometer probably isn't at the top of your list of things to purchase when moving into a new living space. However, if you have kids living with you or young nieces or nephews who may stay over, you'll be glad to have the fast and accurate BD Rapid Flex Digital Thermometer on hand.

Alarm System

When I moved out of my marital home and into my new space as a single guy, one of the first orders of business was to install an inexpensive alarm system. Even though I felt safe in my surroundings, I also recognized there would be people living in my apartment complex whom I'd never met and would likely never get to know. Better to be safe than sorry.

There are many types of home and apartment alarm systems. Since I didn't want to run wires through the walls and ceiling I opted for a wireless system. I also opted for an alarm that didn't come with a monthly monitoring fee, but at the same time was easy to set up, inexpensive, and loud enough to wake me at night if someone did decide to break in.

Skylink Security System Deluxe Kit (SC-100)

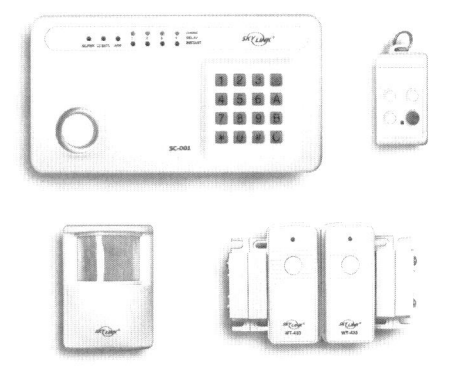

(© Skylink Group at **www.skylinkhome.com**)

After careful research, I purchased the Skylink Security System Deluxe Kit (SC-100). The Skylink SC-100 comes with a control panel, two door or window sensors (the sensors are multi-use – designed to monitor both), a motion sensor, and a keychain transmitter (additional door/window sensors can be purchased as well).

Installation was simple. It took me about three hours to install the entire system and I've been very happy with its performance ever since. I've had zero false alarms and all components of the system have worked flawlessly. In addition, setting and disarming the alarm is very easy – my kids have no difficulty using it.

If you're in a location where a home alarm may be necessary (or if only for peace of mind), I'd recommend giving the Skylink SC-100 system a look – inexpensive, easy to use, and very effective!

Cutlery Set

Upon re-entering bachelorhood I made a promise to myself that I'd improve my cooking skills. At the time of my divorce I could only cook the most basic of meals – and those not very well. Scrambled eggs and homemade pizza were pushing the limits of my culinary abilities.

Victorinox 8-Piece Knife Block Set

(© *Victorinox Swiss Army at* **www.swissarmy.com**)

I knew that an essential requirement for home cooking was having quality cutlery on hand. I didn't want to spend a small fortune but still wanted a cutlery set that would last for years to come.

After reading many Amazon.com reviews, I decided on the Victorinox 8-Piece Knife Block Set. In this set, you get four distinct cutting knives, a slicing knife (which looks like something you could jimmy open a car door with but is instead used for carving roasts, poultry, and the like), kitchen shears, a sharpening steel, and a hardwood block to hold it all together.

The blades are made of quality high-carbon steel, come with a lifetime warranty, and are extremely sharp. The hardwood block is also well made and comes with two extra slots if you decide to add additional knives to your set.

I was so impressed with the Victorinox set that several months later I decided to add to my cutlery family by purchasing the Victorinox Fibrox 7-Inch Granton Edge Santoku Knife. A Granton edge refers to cut-outs along the edge of a knife blade that help keep the food you're cutting from sticking to the blade – I've found this to be very handy when slicing vegetables!

The Granton edge on the Victorinox *Fibrox 7-Inch Santoku Knife*

(© *Victorinox Swiss Army at* **www.swissarmy.com**)

I'm very happy with the Victorinox 8-Piece Knife Block Set and the Fibrox 7-Inch Granton Edge Santoku Knife. I'd heartily recommend them to any guy looking for a quality set of kitchen knives at a reasonable price!

Storage Containers

During my married life, I always seemed to have a difficult time keeping food fresh when it was stored in the cupboards or pantry, mostly due to the outdated mish-mash of storage containers I had on hand. Not only did many of my previous storage containers not work very well, but most were also irritatingly opaque. As a result, I often had to open the containers to determine what was inside.

I vowed I wasn't going to have that particular little heartache when I moved out on my own. My research into storage containers led me to the best containers I've ever used – the OXO Good Grips 10-Piece POP Container Set (the containers are also sold individually, but there's a price break if you buy them in a set).

OXO containers create an airtight seal with their push-button tops and as a result, I've noticed that food stays fresh longer. In addition, they're made of clear, BPA-free plastic so it's effortless to see what's inside. They store and stack easily due to their rectangular base but also look great sitting by themselves on a kitchen counter.

OXO Good Grips 10-Piece POP Container Set

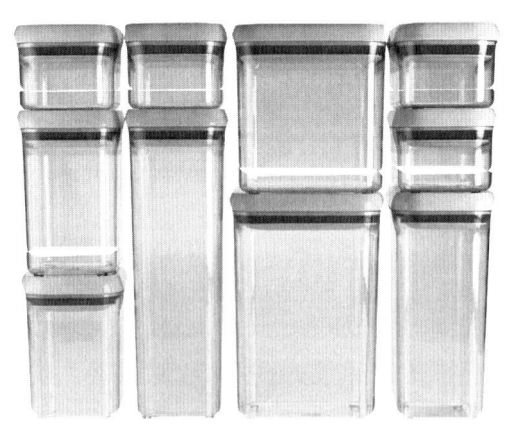

(© *OXO International at **www.oxo.com**)*

Though not inexpensive, OXO containers should give many years of service. You can find them online or at many brick and mortar stores, including BBB (think coupons!).

Dinnerware

Although I already had a nice dinnerware set for my new home, I wanted to get another "fun" set that my kids could use for themselves and their friends. After a bit of searching I landed on Zak Designs plates, bowls, and tumblers.

Zak Designs plates are made of break-resistant melamine and as such, work well for patio dining or outdoor picnics, as well as indoor dining. My kids really enjoy using this colorful tableware (they're always fighting over who gets what color).

I've found the plates have a great adult function as well: the tall lip around the outside of the plates helps keep food and juices from spilling over the edge. For example, Zak Designs plates are great for holding a roast that has been taken from the oven and is "resting" before it is to be cut. When it's time to cut the meat, the lip on the Zak Designs plate will keep the juices on the plate and off the counter and the floor.

Zak Designs 6-Piece Dinner Sets – Plates, Bowls, and Tumblers

(© Zak! Designs at **www.zak.com**)

These plates also work great for single-guy "TV dinners." The tall lip helps prevent your food from sliding off the plate and onto the couch. Zak Designs dinner sets – bringing worry-free, in-front-of-the-TV dining back to its rightful place – a must for single guys everywhere!

Soap Dispenser

During the years I was married, I struggled with having soap at the ready near the kitchen sink. The soap dispenser always seemed to be clogged or broken. I eventually abandoned the soap-dispenser-at-the-kitchen-sink idea because I couldn't find one that would hold up to everyday use. Feeling somewhat defeated, I simply left a bottle of hand soap on the counter near the sink, which always looked a bit out of place.

When I moved into my apartment, I vowed to fix this finicky issue and find a soap dispenser that was both nice looking and suitably robust – something that wouldn't stop working after just a few months of use. I went through several dispensers before landing on the Progressive International Soap Dispenser (sounds rather dignified, no?).

Progressive International Soap Dispenser

(© *Progressive International at www.progressiveintl.com*)

The Progressive dispenser is pleasant to look at, durable, and easy to use. The body of the dispenser has a stylish teardrop shape made of transparent plastic – so it's easy to tell when it needs to be refilled. In addition, the Progressive dispenser has another unique feature: an extra-long spout that hangs over the sink so any drips from the dispenser land there and not on the counter.

If you want a soap dispenser that – dare I say it – looks *sexy*, but is still functional and well built, take a good look at the Progressive International Soap Dispenser!

Tie Rack

If you're like me, you've collected a number of ties that you wear to work, social events, and business functions. Over the years, I've owned several styles of racks to manage and hold these ties. All my old tie racks had one thing in common: they were prone to letting my ties slip off the rack and onto the floor. There just wasn't enough "stickiness" on the rack to hold the ties firmly in place.

Friction Tie Rack and Scarf Hanger – Non-Slip

(© Richards Homewares at **www.richardshomewares.com**)

When I moved out on my own, I found a tie rack that addresses this problem (and does so while still managing to look stylish). It's the Friction Tie Rack and Scarf Hanger! The Friction tie rack has a unique (and so simple it's brilliant) non-slip friction surface that uses a dense sponge-type material to hold each necktie in place. The hanger is made of a durable chrome-plated metal and can hold up to 24 ties.

If you want to keep your ties in the air and off the ground, consider acquiring a Friction Tie Rack and Scarf Hanger for your closet. Your aeronautically challenged ties will thank you!

Laundry Sorter

The Honey-Can-Do Laundry Sorter is one of the few items on my list that I no longer have a need for (due to my housekeeper staying on top of my laundry so effectively – the "why" and "how" of hiring a housekeeper is discussed in detail in the next chapter). However, the fact that I no longer need one doesn't diminish the quality and versatility of the Honey-Can-Do sorter.

Honey-Can-Do Laundry Sorter (SRT01235)

(© *Honey-Can-Do International at* **www.honeycando.com**)

I actually went through several brands of laundry sorters before finding the Honey-Can-Do. The others I tried were not engineered very well and felt flimsy and cheaply made. The Honey-Can-Do, on the other hand, is very sturdy and durable

— and it looks great, too! It has a chrome frame and includes three removable (and washable) cotton bags. The sorter also comes with a limited lifetime warranty.

If you want a laundry sorter that can easily handle everyday use and abuse, and do it with style, consider the Honey-Can-Do Laundry Sorter!

Power Tool

A list of products for guys to use in their home wouldn't be complete without at least one power tool! Of all the items I purchased for my new home, the Skil 7.2v Lithium-Ion Cordless Screwdriver and Drill was by far the most helpful in the early days of getting my new living space together (I originally owned the 2362 model but recently upgraded to the 2364-02 model – both are excellent). I used the Skil cordless screwdriver to hang pictures on the walls, tighten loose hinges and drawer pulls, install a home alarm system, and put together the ready-to-assemble furniture I purchased from IKEA (**www.ikea.com**).

Skil 7.2v Lithium-Ion Cordless Screwdriver and Drill (2364-02)

*(© Robert Bosch Tool Corporation at **www.skiltools.com**)*

If you plan on buying any ready-to-assemble furniture for your new home (that is, furniture that comes in a box that you unpack and assemble yourself), a cordless screwdriver will save you a lot of time (and sore wrists) by eliminating all the manual twisting and turning necessary with an old-fashioned screwdriver.

And because the Skil cordless screwdriver uses a lithium-ion battery (saying "lithium-ion" just sounds cool, doesn't it?), it can run longer on a single charge than a comparable screwdriver with a standard rechargeable battery. Even after being in my apartment for some time, I still use my Skil cordless screwdriver every couple weeks and it's never let me down. Although a little pricey, once you drill down (eh-hem) into the specs, the Skil 7.2v Cordless Screwdriver and Drill is a very worthy investment!

CHAPTER 4

Creating a Female-Friendly Home

Once your living space is set up and functional, the dust has settled on your singleness, and your kids (if any) have become acclimated to their life with the new, single you, the idea of dating will probably enter into your thoughts.

If you're considering dating, chances are good that at some point you're going to bring dates back to your home (if you're looking for dating advice, chapter 11 holds many tips and suggestions). Maybe you'll cook a meal for your date at home, have her over to watch a movie, or simply stop by for a cocktail on the way to an evening out together.

Whatever the reason, odds are good that newfound female acquaintances will be making their way into your home sooner or later. *You'll* be ready to meet them, but will your home?

To be sure it is, take time, *before* you start dating, to make your living space female friendly. Steer clear of having your home look or feel like a "man cave" or bachelor pad. Instead, give a nod to the female element and ensure that your home speaks, at least in part, to your softer side.

A "Maid In" Voyage for Your Home

The first step in creating a female-friendly home is to make sure your home looks and smells great. A clean home is a must when you start dating and meeting new women. If you decide to bring your date back to your place, she *is* going to notice if your living space isn't tidy and up to her standards.

As the saying goes, "Housework is something you do that nobody notices until you don't do it." Make sure you set aside time every week to keep your home looking good. If the burden of cleaning becomes too much or you'd rather spend your time doing other things, hiring out the work may be something to consider.

When I first set out as a single guy, hiring a housekeeper was a foreign concept. When I was married, my ex had performed most of the housekeeping duties, including the laundry. The magnitude of this particular change hit home after just a few weeks of living single: keeping the apartment clean was turning into a real time sink – it was taking me over five hours every week just to keep things tidy and clean.

Because I had a parenting and work schedule that didn't afford me the luxury of seeing my children every day, I wanted to make sure the time I *did* have with my kids was spent focused on them. In addition, when I wasn't working and didn't have my kids with me, I wanted to spend my time pursuing new interests like cooking, writing, and meeting new and interesting people.

In short, I wanted to save as much time as possible for my kids and myself and jettison anything that took away from those two focal points. However, I had to reconcile this with the fact that I'd be tasked with doing *more* things for myself, not less, in my newly single life. This included making home-cooked meals, house cleaning, and doing the laundry.

I enjoyed the thought of cooking and wanted to teach myself (and my kids) how to create healthy home-cooked meals – so I decided that this was something I would "keep on my plate."

Contrary to cooking, however, cleaning and doing laundry were *not* favorite activities – not even in the top 30 – but they still had to get done. After some consideration, I decided that doing the laundry and cleaning the apartment were two things I could delegate to someone else. For the first time in my life, I decided to bring a maid into my home.

You may feel that a housekeeper is an unneeded expense. I did as well until I took a hard look at the cost of hiring a housekeeper vs. what my time was worth, and considered the potential monetary and time savings. To perform this analysis, I took out a sheet of paper and created a worksheet to objectively review the costs vs. benefits.

Here's what I came up with:

	5 Hours of Cleaning per Week	7.5 Hours of Cleaning per Week
Lost Wages per Month:	$500	$750
Lost Hours per Month:	20	30
Housekeeper Cost per Month:	$250	$250
Monetary Savings per Month:	$500 – $250 = $250	$750 – $250 = $500
Time Saved per Month:	20	30

If you're not a math wizard – no worries – the calculations are very simple. For starters, let's assume you make $50,000 a year at your job – that's roughly $25 an hour ($50,000 / 2080 work hours in a year). You now need to estimate how much time per week you're going to spend cleaning your home and doing the laundry.

I spent about 5 hours per week working on laundry and cleaning the apartment. To keep things simple, let's use 5 hours as the estimate for the time it would take you to clean your home and work on laundry every week as well – 5 hours per week * $25 an hour is $125 a week. This means that your time, viewed from a "what you could make if you were working instead of cleaning and doing laundry" perspective, would be worth $125 a week or $500 a month ($125 a week * 4 weeks). Put $500 and 20 hours (5 hours per week * 4 weeks) in the Lost Wages per Month and Lost Hours per Month boxes, respectively.

As you can see from the worksheet, the potential benefits of hiring a housekeeper include both monetary and time savings. Lost Wages per Month represents the wages you might lose if you were cleaning your home instead of working. And Lost Hours per Month represents the amount of free time you could lose by doing housework instead of other activities. For example, instead of working in your home cleaning, you could spend your Lost Hours per Month at the park with your kids, developing your freelance photography skills, volunteering at a local charity, or meeting new and interesting people at social events.

Now let's look at the other side of the coin – the monetary cost of hiring a housekeeper. I found a fantastic housekeeper, Donna, through a good friend's recommendation. Donna spends, on average, about 4 hours per week cleaning my apartment and doing the laundry (Donna is much faster at cleaning than I could ever be – where it would take me 5 hours she can get even more work done in 4). For the 16 hours per month Donna spends at my apartment, I pay her $15 an hour, or approximately $250 a month (16 hours per month * $15 an hour).

Since Donna is an excellent, real-world example we'll use what I'm spending on Donna in our worksheet – that's $250 in the Housekeeper Cost per Month box. For illustrative purposes, a second column is included showing the analysis for 7.5 hours of cleaning per week (e.g. maybe you're a bit slower with your cleaning – keeping an eye on the latest sports scores while vacuuming and dusting), but keeping Donna at the same 16 hours per month.

At this point, you need only perform a simple calculation to objectively determine your potential monetary and time savings for hiring a housekeeper. Take Lost Wages per Month and subtract Housekeeper Cost per Month to come up with your Monetary Savings per Month. Your Time Saved per Month is the same as your Lost Hours per Month.

In our example, if you cleaned and worked on laundry by yourself you'd be losing out on making $500 a month (Lost Wages per Month). However, if you hired Donna at $250 a month you could then work the hours you would've spent cleaning and doing laundry to make an additional $250 a month. You're actually in the positive an additional $250 per month ($500 in extra wages per month - $250 spent on Donna) by hiring Donna!

> To aid you in your analysis of whether or not to hire a housekeeper, a spreadsheet containing the same formulas used here is posted on the Single Effort website at **www.SingleEffort.com/free**. You can download the spreadsheet and run the numbers for your own situation.

If money is not as important to you or you don't work at a job that pays hourly, you can also ask yourself this question: "What is my time worth?" If you have kids, is spending $15 an hour to be with them a worthwhile investment? If you don't have children, is $15 an hour something you're willing to pay to free up your time to follow an endeavor or hobby you've always wanted to pursue?

Of course, only you can answer these questions. The goal is to help you lay out the numbers objectively so that you can make your own decision based on your particular needs and objectives.

One final note on cleaning – sometimes it's the little things that can trip you up before your date arrives. Things like leaving a toilet seat up, forgetting to wipe down the kitchen counters, failing to light a few nice-smelling candles, or forgetting to check if there's enough toilet paper left on the roll (requiring a certain degree of finesse to alleviate if your date is already in the bathroom).

In the whirlwind of activity before your date arrives, things can get overlooked! A handy "Date Night Checklist" can help keep you on track and ensure that nothing is missed before her arrival.

> The Single Effort Date Night Checklist is available for you to download. Visit **www.SingleEffort.com/free** to access your own ready-to-use checklist.

The Inverse Cleaning Theory of Hotness

If you decide to hire a maid, and it's a female, steer clear of using this as an opportunity to find a "hot" housekeeper. Most guys have fantasies of a beautiful French maid in a low-cut blouse and miniskirt working in their home. However, keep your wits about you and remember that this is a person you're inviting into your sanctuary and who could be in contact with your kids, if you have any.

Chapter 4: Creating a Female-Friendly Home   61

You don't want looks to be the deciding factor for whether you bring someone into your home (well, at least as it relates to housekeeping!). "Wipe away" those French maid fantasies and leave the low-cut blouse and miniskirt for the right date instead.

When looking for a maid, you may also want to consider the somewhat controversial Single Effort theory on housekeepers. It holds that the cleaning ability of a housekeeper is inversely proportional to her attractiveness. That is, as a woman's "hotness" goes up, her cleaning ability declines.

According to this theory, a woman who's very good looking is probably someone who has relied on her looks (at least in part) throughout her life, and as a cute woman, may not clean as well as someone who hasn't relied on her looks and instead relies solely on her cleaning abilities.

The Inverse Cleaning Theory of Hotness

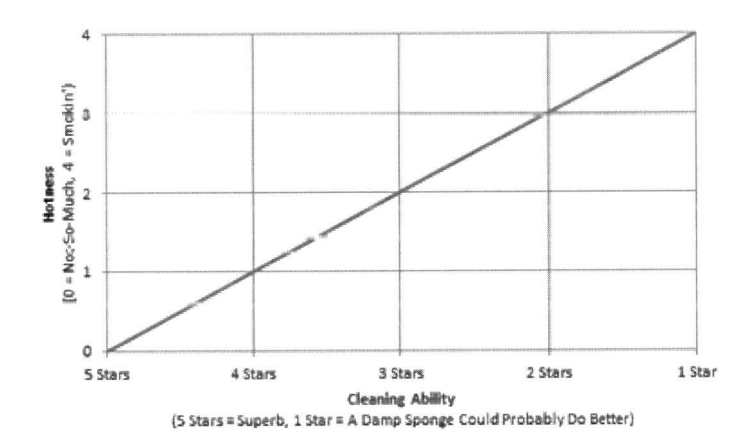

Of course, there are going to be exceptions. You may find a nice looking housekeeper who does a super job cleaning. Donna happens to be a nice looking woman but I hired her strictly for her cleaning abilities, based solely on glowing recommendations.

When it comes to finding the right housekeeper for you, one of the best ways is through friends and family. But if you don't have referrals to narrow the field, you can visit craigslist and search in the "services offered" section for the key words "housekeeper" or "maid." If you're not familiar with craigslist you can think of it as an online version of the classifieds section of a newspaper. However, unlike the newspaper, posting and viewing items and services for sale on craigslist are (in most cases) completely free.

If you decide to interview for housekeepers, try to get at least three references from past or current employers for each candidate you interview. This will help you make sure that your housekeeper, hot or not, can actually clean.

And finally, shy away from hiring someone to clean your home who also has ties to your ex – like a common friend, a family member, or a housekeeper who might already be working for your ex. If you're newly single, your ex is going to be interested in knowing how you're adapting to your new life – if you're dating, who you're dating, and what you're doing in your free time. If you hire someone who also knows or has ties to her, you run the risk of having your housekeeper (intentionally or not) giving your ex details about your single life that you'd most likely want to keep private.

A Slice of Pizza with That Dry Cleaning?

Regardless of whether you employ a housekeeper to handle your laundry or do it yourself, it's likely you'll still have clothes that will require dry cleaning. Although we all enjoy the end result of using a dry cleaner's services (e.g. neatly pressed shirts and slacks) most of us dislike the pilgrimage to the cleaners to drop off and pick up our laundry.

I often felt like I could be doing something more productive than driving to and from my dry cleaner every week for clean clothes. On a whim one day, I decided to call around to see if any cleaners near me offered pick-up and drop-off services. Surprisingly, several did – and for the same price I was paying to drop off and pick up my own clothes!

At first, I thought a pick-up and drop-off laundry service seemed like an odd concept – something that should only be reserved for the wealthy. Then I realized I'd been living in the stone ages. How many people still drive to pick up a pizza? If we have the technology to deliver a piping hot pizza, surely we can do the same for cold clothes!

Since this small but significant finding, I now leave my dirty clothes outside in a laundry bag, hanging on a hook installed near the front door. Once a week my dry cleaner picks up the dirty clothes and drops off the clean – hanging the clean clothes neatly on the same hook (encased in a clear plastic bag to protect them from the elements).

Once you've located a dry cleaning service that will pick up and drop off your laundry, have a little celebration and treat yourself to some pizza – delivered, of course!

Field-Tested Cleaning Products That Work!

Even if you decide to hire a housekeeper, there will still be many occasions when you'll need to clean things on your own. Maybe it's a young child's budding artistry drawn on a bedroom wall, a dropped plate of spaghetti, or a mud room that's, well, muddy. To help keep your home looking and smelling great, you'll want to use products with exceptional cleaning abilities that deliver the best value for your hard-earned money.

As mentioned earlier, one upside of my marriage was that my ex did most of the household cleaning. So when I moved out on my own and it came time to purchase cleaning products, I was a bit dazed by all the choices – have you ever stepped back and taken a look at the sheer variety of products in the household cleaning aisle of your local supermarket or grocery store?

To meet this challenge I leveraged the same method I'd used earlier, relying on actual consumer feedback via Consumer Reports and Amazon.com, but also field-tested recommendations from Donna, my housekeeper, and my own trial and error. The result was a set of cleaning products, itemized on the following pages, that have earned the Single Effort cleaning seal of approval.

With cleaning products, the adage "you get what you pay for" is usually true – in my experience less expensive generics often don't clean as well as their name-brand equivalents. To make cleaning as effortless as possible, I try to stick to name-brand products. However, if you prefer using generics you can find them for just about every cleaning product listed in this section (note that items marked with a * are reviewed following the list).

Chapter 4: Creating a Female-Friendly Home   65

The Single Effort list of recommended household cleaning products:

All-Purpose Cleaner (Eco-Friendly)
GREEN WORKS® All-Purpose Cleaner

(© 2012 The Clorox Company. Reprinted with permission. GREEN WORKS is a registered trademark of The Clorox Company)

Bathroom Cleaner
Soft Scrub with Bleach Cleanser

(© Henkel Consumer Goods, Inc. at www.henkelna.com)

Dish Scrubber Sponge *
Magic Jetz Scrubz

(© Harold Import Co. at www.haroldimport.com)

Dish Soap
Ajax Lemon

(© Colgate-Palmolive at www.colgatepalmolive.com)

Dryer Sheets
Bounce Free (No Dyes or Perfumes)

(© Procter & Gamble at www.pg.com)

Glass Cleaner
Sprayway Glass Cleaner

(© Sprayway, Inc. at www.spraywayinc.com)

66   SINGLE EFFORT

"Goo" Remover *
Goo Gone

(© Homax Products at
www.homaxproducts.com)

Laundry Detergent
Tide 2x Ultra with a Touch of Downy

(© Procter & Gamble at **www.pg.com**)

Magical Cleaning Pads *
Mr. Clean Magic Eraser

(© Procter & Gamble at **www.pg.com**)

Multi-Purpose Cleaner
Greased Lightning Multi-Purpose Cleaner

(© Chemtura at **www.chemtura.com**.
Reprinted with permission from Chemtura
Corporation. All rights reserved.)

Stainless Steel Cleaner
Sprayway #841 Stainless Steel Polish and Cleaner

(© Sprayway, Inc. at
www.spraywayinc.com)

Stainless Steel Cookware Cleaner *
Bar Keepers Friend

(© Servaas Labs at
www.barkeepersfriend.com)

Toilet Bowl and Bathroom Cleaner Scratch-Free Comet Lemon Fresh with Bleach

Toilet Bowl Plunger * Cobra E-Z Plunger

(© The Spic and Span Company at **www.cometcleanser.com**)

(© Cobra US at **www.cobraus.com**)

Many of the cleaning products listed above are self-explanatory. However, a few are worth further comment:

Bar Keepers Friend

Bar Keepers Friend is the best product I've found for cleaning stainless steel cookware. If you own stainless steel pots and pans (a discussion on the merits of stainless steel cookware follows in the next chapter), then you owe it to yourself to pick up a can of Bar Keepers Friend. Used with an S.O.S. steel wool pad, Bar Keepers Friend works wonders on stainless steel cookware, removing the blemishes that make their way onto pots and pans and returning them to like-new condition.

Bar Keepers Friend is also great at removing rust and hard water stains from copper, tile, brass, marble, and porcelain. The folks making Bar Keepers Friend must be doing something right – the product has been around since the 1880s!

Goo Gone

Goo Gone is one of those products you don't think you'll ever need – until you need it. Goo Gone excels at removing, well, goo. From grease and oil, to tar and crayon, Goo Gone is one of the best "oops" fixer products on the market.

I use Goo Gone whenever I need to spot treat a grease stain on clothing or when I need to remove tape or price sticker residue from a store bought item. As a nice by-product, Goo Gone also has a pleasant citrus aroma – no toxic chemical smell. I keep Goo Gone at the ready in my house. I recommend keeping a bottle in your house as well.

Magic Jetz Scrubz

Prior to being single, I remember my dish scrubbers falling apart or losing their effectiveness after just a few uses. After moving into my apartment, I searched online in an effort to remedy this particular inconvenience. I came across rave reviews for the Magic Jetz Scrubz scrubber sponge. I ordered a couple Magic Jetz Scrubz scrubbers (say that five times fast) and can say these are indeed the best dish and pan scrubbers I've used.

These scrubbers won't scratch your cookware and they're very wear-and-tear resistant. They're made of a unique scratch-free material that feels like a synthetic version of an S.O.S. pad.

The synthetic material allows a Jetz Scrubz scrubber to last for months before it needs to be replaced.

In addition, Jetz Scrubz scrubbers are dishwasher safe. To "renew" your scrubber simply place it in the top rack of your dishwasher for a wash cycle. Consider picking up a couple Magic Jetz Scrubz for your kitchen and create some cleaning magic of your own!

Mr. Clean Magic Eraser
With kids in the house I'm constantly finding new scuffmarks on the walls, floor, and doors. On a friend's recommendation, I used a Mr. Clean Magic Eraser on these pesky marks and found they disappeared with little effort. My housekeeper, Donna, swears by Magic Erasers as well (well, sometimes *at* them too – when she comes across a fresh scuffmark that requires her immediate attention.)

And the Mr. Clean Magic Eraser isn't just for scuffmarks, but for pencil marks and all manner of blemishes on walls, floors, and doors. If you have small children, these are a must!

Note: This is one cleaning product where I deviate from my preference of sticking to name-brand products – here I often use a generic instead. You can find no-name sponges with the same cleaning attributes as a Mr. Clean Magic Eraser on eBay for much less. Simply search eBay for the keywords "magic eraser" or "magic sponge" and see what appears!

Cobra E-Z Plunger

The plunger. Another product you'll never know you need – until you need it. And if you don't have it when you need it, you'll wish you did. I once had an issue with a self-induced toilet bowl clog that occurred two hours before a date was to arrive at my apartment. I couldn't get the toilet to flush (most likely due to the disproportionate amount of beef I'd eaten the night before). The Cobra E-Z Plunger saved me from some noteworthy embarrassment!

The E-Z plunger is lightweight and made with a bellows-type design that delivers more pressure than a typical cup plunger. In addition, it's small and stores "E-Z-ly" under a bathroom sink.

The E-Z Plunger can be found online and in most big-name hardware and home improvement stores. When you need a plunger, you definitely *need* a plunger. Don't be caught with your pants down – keep the Cobra E-Z plunger handy in your home and you'll never have to worry about being "flushed" with embarrassment!

Some Do's and Don'ts

Making time to keep your living space clean, while good for you (and if you have children, setting a great example for them), will also pay off when you decide to bring dates into your home. Many dates and girl+friends have assured me that a guy who keeps a clean home is a rarity in today's dating world. If you do your best to keep your living space clean and tidy, it'll definitely give you an edge on your dating competition.

But there's more to making your home female friendly than just keeping it clean. You'll also need to give a nod to your softer side and make sure your home is inviting in other ways. If a woman is put off by your home – if it's not warm and inviting to her when she visits – then whether it's clean or dirty won't matter, she simply won't care to return. And all the work you've put into developing a connection with her could be lost.

Creating an inviting atmosphere in your home where women feel welcome and comfortable will hopefully require just a few small changes. No wholesale or expensive modifications needed – just a few simple Do's and Don'ts:

DO try to keep the décor and overall mood in your home modern and upbeat. My ability and experience in decorating starts and stops at zero. In the immortal words of Dirty Harry, "A man's got to know his limitations." So when it came time to decorate my apartment, I promptly sought advice from two girl+friends. They helped me make my living space female friendly, picking out the proper accessories to liven it up while at the same time toning down the testosterone.

Not sure what would be considered modern or what might constitute upbeat? Take the opportunity to Single Effort educating yourself while at the same time creating an inviting atmosphere in your home – ask several of your girl+friends over for an informal advice session on home décor.

As an added perk, when you involve your girl+friends in decorating your home, it'll put them on notice that you're serious about meeting new women and making a good impression. They'll tell their friends about your new place and the word will spread – making it known that you have style and taste in decorating (and possibly leading to new dates for you as a result!).

DON'T hang pictures of scantily clad women on the walls, and keep that velvet picture of Elvis in storage. Instead, use pictures, prints, and wall art that are warm and inviting, yet still make a statement about you. You don't have to spend a lot of time looking for pictures and prints to hang on your walls, either. A quick trip online or to your local home goods store can net you some nice prints quickly.

If you don't have a lot of money to spend, consider visiting your local resale shop or second-hand store. Or spend a day picking up items for your home by visiting yard sales in your area (probably best to pass over any GI Joe action figures, though – unless you have young kids at home and can pass them off as theirs!). Oftentimes, wall art found at yard sales will be in great shape and priced ridiculously low.

Just because something is inexpensive doesn't mean it looks any less nice. I've found several great prints at my local Walmart and Target for under $20. In fact, two prints hanging in my master bathroom were purchased for a grand total of $6 – but they look great! Don't focus on spending a lot of money. Focus instead on décor that makes a statement about you and speaks, at least in part, to your softer side.

DO make sure, if you have kids, that you have their pictures hanging up in your home as well. Not only will it make your children feel special and more comfortable but it also reinforces to any dates you bring over that you're a package deal. Anyone interested in you must also be willing to invest in your children.

In addition, most women respect a guy who's also a great dad – and having your kid's pictures prominently displayed will emphasize to your dates that you place a great deal of importance on your relationship with your children.

DON'T put up pictures of past girlfriends or your ex in the main living areas of your home. This will only broadcast the message that you're not yet over your past relationships. Instead, put up pictures of you and your friends. Choose some of your best pictures that showcase your fun-loving side – without pictures of past relationships anywhere nearby.

If you have children, pictures of their mom are fine but they should stay in the children's rooms. Areas like the living room, family room, kitchen, and dining room should remain "past-relationship-free."

DO buy a few nice-smelling candles to use in your home. Consider placing a candle in the living room and one in the bathroom or guest bathroom. If you have a date coming to your home, light the candles at least 30 minutes before your date is to arrive. The candles will fill your home with a pleasant aroma and give your date a great first impression when she walks in the door.

Part of being a Good Knight is anticipating your date's wants and desires. If romance is in the air and passion leads to the bedroom, a candle there is also a welcome touch and will enhance the romantic atmosphere.

If you need to buy candles, consider purchasing soy candles instead of traditional paraffin wax candles. Soy candles are beneficial for several reasons:

- Soy candles generally burn cleaner than paraffin candles and produce very little black soot. You won't find black lines on walls or objects nearby when a soy candle is burning.
- Soy candles tend to burn slower. A good soy candle can burn up to twice as long as a similar-size paraffin candle.
- Soy is also a renewable and cost-effective resource, made from the soybean plant. Because much of our soybean consumption is from soybeans grown in the United States, using soy candles benefits the American agricultural economy.

To get the full benefit of soy candles you should look for ones that say "100% Soy" rather than settling for a soy blend. If you can't find soy candles locally, turn to online shopping where you'll find a vast selection. I order soy candles from the Zionsville Candle Company (**www.zionsvillecandlecompany.com**). In fact, I liked their candles so much I became a member of their candle of the month club – a pair of new soy candles was delivered to my home monthly (yes, it's OK for guys to like candles. Just don't go too far – taking up scrapbooking is probably stepping over the line!).

Soy candles burn cleaner, last longer, and benefit American agriculture – definitely Single Effort approved!

DON'T forget to accessorize. The phrase "home accessory" might sound a bit feminine and cause many guys to run for cover. However, the truth is that adding a few inexpensive decorative items to your home can do a lot to make your living space look both stylish and inviting. A throw pillow or two on top of the couch or the bed, a nice rug in the living room, a mirror hung properly in the hallway, or even a few stand-alone light fixtures can all help make your home more appealing and inviting to your female guests.

DO place a couple live plants and flowers in your home. Not only do plants and flowers look nice and smell good but they also speak to women. Plants and flowers in your home say, "Hey, I'm a multifaceted guy! I enjoy many things besides ESPN and the occasional trip to Home Depot!"

Fresh-cut plants and flowers are relatively inexpensive and well worth the minimal upkeep (tips for caring for plants and flowers are right around the corner in the next section). They brighten the ambiance of any room and are a magnet for pleasant conversation.

Flowers at home are great for Good Knight moments as well. If you have a date coming to your home, surprise her by taking a fresh flower from its vase and giving it to her at the door!

Your Plants and Flowers – May They Live Long & Prosper

Regardless of whether you purchase flowers from the grocery store or florist, or pick them yourself, all flowers will live longer if you know how to care for them. Here are several tips you can follow to keep your flowers looking and smelling great:

Minimize the amount of time the flowers are out of water after you purchase or pick them. If possible, transport the flowers to your home with their stems immersed in water.

When you get your flowers home, find a vase or vessel to hold them. Nothing fancy is required – a small, clear vase can be had for less than $5 at your local supermarket (a 24-ounce Tervis Tumbler also works great). Ensure the vessel holding your flowers is clean and fill it with lukewarm water mixed with the proper amount of fresh flower food (normally available where flowers are purchased). Commercial flower food really does help extend the life of flowers by several days. If you don't have commercial flower food handy, substitute with a pinch of sugar.

Before you place the flowers in their vase, remove ½" to 1" from the bottom of the stem of each flower. Be sure to cut the stems at an angle to expose maximum surface area of the stem – this helps the flowers absorb their needed water. Also, use a pair of sharp scissors. Using dull scissors can compress the stems, destroying the vessels that transport the water and preventing proper water absorption. Once the stems are cut, place the flowers in their vase and enjoy!

Your flowers will require a small amount of ongoing TLC. Every other day, remove them from their vase and recut the stems at an angle with a pair of sharp scissors – again, removing ½" to 1" of stem. While the flowers are still out of their vase, dump out the old water and replace with lukewarm water mixed with the proper amount of fresh flower food or a pinch of sugar (changing the water regularly helps prevent the growth of bacteria which can damage flowers). Place the flowers back in their clean vase and relish your green thumb handiwork!

Flowers are great female-friendly accessories for your home. Their only downside is that they're like the Redshirt characters from a classic *Star Trek* episode – i.e. they need to be replaced regularly (Redshirts are the nameless, easily forgotten characters that turn up in the original *Star Trek* TV series – they're expendable and regularly killed off to dramatize dangerous situations). Consider minimizing the work required to keep vibrant flora in your home by placing a couple small indoor plants in your living space as well.

Indoor plants live much longer than fresh-cut flowers and they help clean and freshen the air in your home. Try to place your plants near windows in your main living areas – like your dining room, family room, or kitchen – locations where they can be viewed by you and your guests and at the same time receive adequate natural sunlight.

Unless you have time to spend working with your plants every day, focus on plants that do well in mid to low light conditions and require minimal care. After research and experimentation, I've found that the following low-light-friendly plants do very well in my apartment for months on end:

Massangeana Cane ~ Cyclamen ~ Aglaonema Emerald Beauty

(© ShutterStock at **www.shutterstock.com**)

If these names might as well be written in Klingon, consider visiting your local nursery and asking for assistance. They'll most likely carry these plants along with other low-light-friendly / low-maintenance flora that will be ideal for your home.

Please also note that not all plants need to be located in your main living areas. On a recommendation from a girl+friend, I purchased a single-stem orchid that I placed in my guest bathroom. It brings a bit of stylishness and refinement to the room – something I think we all could use in that particular space!

Single-Stem Orchid

(© ShutterStock at **www.shutterstock.com**)

If you decide to populate your home with plants and flowers, save yourself some grief and purchase a small watering can. Why bother with such a seemingly simple device? Because without a watering can handy, you'll likely choose the path of least resistance to water your greenery. That means grabbing whatever is handy – usually it's a drinking glass – and inevitably spilling water all over as you fumble to pour from it.

After going this route myself (and then wiping up the resulting water spills for what seemed like the hundredth time), I purchased an inexpensive plastic watering can that's small enough to store easily and does its job without muss or fuss. You can find your own at most grocery or hardware stores – Ikea sells them as well for as little as a dollar.

And unless you happen to be playing the part of a Redshirt character in an upcoming *Star Trek* episode, you'll probably want to keep your plants and flowers around as long as possible. Spock, the venerable character from the same series, always closed a goodbye with the Vulcan tradition of wishing his friends a long and healthy life, consisting of a hand gesture in the shape of a "V" along with the phrase, "Live long and prosper."

By following a few simple tips, you can ensure a similar fate for your plants and flowers – may they too live long and prosper!

CHAPTER 5

You're Cooking Now!

As you begin to meet new women and enter the dating scene (dating advice is forthcoming in chapter 11), you'll need to find ways to set yourself apart from the other men your date has met. Most women adore a guy who can prepare a well-flavored home-cooked meal, so learning to cook will serve you well.

A nice way to impress a date is to tell her you know how to cook – a better way to impress a date is to *show* her that you *can* cook. Simply understanding a few basics – proper preparation, a few cooking tools, and some essential ingredients – will set you worlds apart from your dating competition, giving her all the incentive she needs to come back for seconds!

Regardless of whether you're a cooking neophyte or already comfortable in the kitchen and just looking for some additional pointers – this chapter is chock full of culinary know-how that will help you stand out from your peers and feed yourself (and others) very well in the process.

Roll up those sleeves and don the apron, it's "thyme" for some "sage" cooking advice!

Getting Started

If you're new to cooking, start by getting familiar with the basics. Cooking websites and TV shows are a great place to start. Did you know they have an entire network on TV devoted to food and cooking? It's called the Food Network (no mystery there), and most cable and dish broadcasters carry it on their standard channel list (they're on the Internet, too, at **www.foodnetwork.com**). Another notable source of cooking lore is America's Test Kitchen (**www.americastestkitchen.com**), a show hosted by Christopher Kimball, editor-in-chief of *Cook's Illustrated* magazine (**www.cooksillustrated.com**).

You can pick up a stunning array of tips and recipes from cooking shows. If it's too overwhelming at first, simply pick one show that interests you and follow it for a few weeks.

Another way to learn about cooking is to look up interesting or fun-sounding recipes and gain a general understanding of the ingredients they require. For finding great recipes online, a popular stop is Allrecipes (**www.allrecipes.com**).

Allrecipes is one of the top recipe sites on the Internet. They're immensely popular for several reasons:

- Their recipes are well organized into food categories and include colorful pictures of the finished meal along with real-world user ratings.
- They allow you to save recipes found on their site into your own virtual recipe box. Once saved, you can look up a recipe with just a few clicks of the mouse.
- They give you the option of printing your recipes, so when you're ready to hit the kitchen you'll have the recipe right in front of you in an easy-to-read format.

Allrecipes is to cooking what Amazon is to shopping. Consider Allrecipes when you're looking for fantastic meal suggestions and exciting new cooking ideas.

Watching others cook and reading through websites and recipes are both good entry points into cooking, but the only way to really learn how to cook is to take a hands-on approach. Simply get into the kitchen and start experimenting. Keep in mind that there are no sacred cows in cooking – everything is open to testing and change. Indeed, as an enterprising individual once said, "Sacred cows make the best hamburgers."

If you're new to cooking, a great way to jump-start your culinary education is to attend a cooking class. You can find many businesses and individuals offering cooking classes near you through a quick search on the Internet. Community colleges and adult education facilities usually offer cooking courses as well.

As an added incentive, attending a cooking class is an excellent way to Single Effort learning a new skill while meeting like-minded single women!

Meez Ahn Plahs, Please

One of the reasons many guys put off learning how to cook is that they believe cooking is time consuming – but the reality is quite the opposite. Sure, it might take a little longer to cook a nice casserole than to pick up the phone and order Chinese takeout. But when you factor in the drive time to and from the restaurant to pick up a takeout meal vs. the time needed to cook a great-tasting dinner, there really isn't much of a time difference (and as a nice side benefit, cooking your own meals is generally healthier and better for your diet).

The key to quick, healthy, and enjoyable cooking is fresh food and just a little up-front planning.

Try to use fresh ingredients whenever possible – this is one of the best ways to ensure you stay healthy and that your meals are packed with flavor. If your recipe calls for carrots or green beans, try to use fresh vegetables from your local grocer (or grown yourself, if you have the time and space). Canned or frozen vegetables simply aren't as flavorful – but they certainly work if fresh isn't available or you're pressed for time.

When shopping for fresh ingredients, keep in mind that grocery stores are a great place to Single Effort meeting new women! I've found the best time to meet new women at grocery stores is Friday evenings. It's during that time that the stores I frequent seem to be full of single females, possibly tired of the Friday night dating scene and shopping to stock up for the following week.

As a side benefit, you'll find that many of the single women you meet in grocery stores will be more open to talking with you than if you'd met them in a bar or at a social event. This is due, in part, to the "Grocery Cart Effect" – the grocery cart you're pushing acts as an indirect barrier between the two of you, giving the woman a sense of security and comfort that makes it easier for her to open up to a conversation.

After you have all your ingredients, but before you start cooking, lay out and prepare everything needed to create the meal. The term for this, *mise en place* (pronounced "meez ahn plahs"), is French for "putting into place" or "all in place." It's the act of having all the ingredients for a meal prepared and at hand, in a well-organized fashion, before you start to cook.

Mise en place is very important in preparing a great-tasting meal, so much so that Anthony Bourdain, a popular celebrity and culinary master who's famous for "telling it like it is", often quotes it as his "religion" when cooking.

No need to get religious – just a little mise en place, *please!*

(© iStockphoto.com)

For example, if you're using garlic in your meal, have the garlic cloves already prepared – peeled, chopped, and placed in a small bowl – prior to cooking the meal itself. You wouldn't start changing the oil in your car before you had the new oil and filter handy, would you? By the same token, make sure you have all the ingredients necessary and all your prep work done before you start cooking your meal.

> *I found a fantastic set of small bowls that are ideal for mise en place cooking. They're the Bormioli Rocco Quattor Stagioni Dipping Bowls (yeah – I know – but I didn't name them). These*

small glass bowls are great to use for mise en place because they don't take up much room on the counter, they're easy to clean and dishwasher safe, and they have perfectly sized handles that make picking them up a breeze.

Each bowl can hold about 8 ounces – which is an ideal size for spices or chopped ingredients that are going to be used in a meal. These bowls are really useful for their stated purpose as well – as dipping bowls for finger foods – and are elegant enough to be used by your guests at parties or social events.

Bormioli Rocco Quattor Stagioni Dipping Bowls

(© *Bormioli Rocco USA at **www.bormioliroccousa.com**)*

A Basic Kitchen Setup, Minus the Plywood

When you have all your ingredients in place and ready to go, you'll need the proper cooking equipment to make the meal happen. Cooking, like anything else, is easier when you have the right tools. Just like most of us would prefer ripping a 4x8 sheet of plywood with an electric circular saw rather than a handsaw, so too, in cooking, the right tools make all the difference.

Fortunately, you don't need a kitchen stocked with expensive or fancy gear to cook most meals. You can cook a wide variety of wonderful meals with just a few simple and inexpensive cooking tools.

As a single guy looking for a basic kitchen setup, you should consider having the following tools on hand:

- Seven (or more) piece cookware set consisting of pots and pans of various sizes.
- Sharp kitchen knives
- Cutting board
- Mixing bowls
- Plastic or wooden utensils
- Measuring cups and spoons
- Electric mixer

With these tools in your kitchen, you can cook just about anything – and set your gastronomic wild side free to explore the many tastes and flavors of the varied meals you'll prepare!

The most important tool in any kitchen is a quality cookware set – consisting of various sizes of pots and pans that are designed to be used both on the stove and in the oven. Cookware is generally produced in two broad categories: non-stick and stainless steel. Ever since the appearance of non-stick cookware on the cooking scene many years ago, there has been a healthy debate on the pros and cons of each.

Non-stick pans have an outer coating of Teflon (or a similar chemical substance) that provides a slippery barrier between the pan and the food. As a point of reference, most professional kitchens use non-stick pans, but in a limited fashion, because the non-stick coating is susceptible to scratching from spatulas, forks, knives, and other metal utensils.

Stainless steel, on the other hand, is a durable metal that doesn't have an outer coating and is not easily susceptible to scratches and scrapes. Because of their durability, stainless steel pans are a staple found in most restaurants and many home kitchens.

However, as with everything in life there are two sides to this story. On the pro side for non-stick cookware, it's generally easier to clean than stainless steel. Bar Keepers Friend, (reviewed in chapter 4) however, does a fantastic job cleaning stainless steel cookware – the only way to improve on this stellar product would be if it came attached to a real barkeeper.

Your personal Barkeeper's Friend – if only!

(© iStockphoto.com)

Also, in theory, you should use less grease when cooking on a non-stick surface since you're only adding oil and butter for taste – not to prevent the food from sticking to the pan.

On the downside, however, any non-stick surface will eventually wear out and need to be replaced. In addition, as already mentioned, you'll need to use plastic or wooden utensils with non-stick cookware because metal will damage the non-stick surface. And the final downside to non-stick cookware? Well, where do you think all those little particles of non-stickiness go when they come off the cookware? Unfortunately, they may find their way into your food.

There are also studies that show some non-stick coatings can be harmful at high temperatures. At extreme temperatures (e.g. near the smoke point of vegetable oils), the non-stick coating on some cookware can break down and release toxic fumes. Stainless steel doesn't have such drawbacks and is the product of choice where high heat is needed (for example, putting a quick sear on the outside of a steak). And as an added benefit, stainless steel is considered a very durable metal – it's resistant to dings and dents and shouldn't pit or corrode.

I used non-stick cookware for 13 years before striking out on my own. It worked fine but the non-stick coating did indeed wear out and flake off over time. As a result, I went through three sets of non-stick cookware during that time. When I transitioned into my single life, I decided to expand my horizons and invest in a quality set of stainless steel cookware. I did my homework on Amazon.com and purchased the Cuisinart Multiclad Pro Stainless Steel 12-Piece Cookware Set.

The pots and pans in the Cuisinart Multiclad Pro cookware set are made from heavy-duty 18/10 stainless steel, and each item has a feel of "heft" and quality to it. The set is fully dishwasher safe and has no plastic pieces to break off or melt (so it works equally well in the oven or on the stove). In addition, the handles stay cool when the pan or pot is on the stovetop and the lids fit snugly (and are interchangeable among several of the pots and pans in the set).

Cuisinart Multiclad Pro Stainless Steel 12-Piece Cookware Set

(© *Cuisinart at* **www.cuisinart.com**)

Buying a good stainless steel cookware set generally represents more of an investment than buying a non-stick cookware set and true to form, the Cuisinart set could set you back close to $300. However, you can easily spend over $1,000 on quality stainless steel cookware, and so comparatively, the Cuisinart set is a relative bargain – and possibly the last cookware set you'll ever need to purchase.

If you need new cookware, deciding whether to purchase a non-stick or stainless steel set will depend on your priorities. If convenience is an important factor, you don't cook very often (or you do but rarely cook with high heat), and you don't mind replacing your cookware every couple years, then non-stick pots and pans might be the right choice for you. Their non-stickiness does work well with "light" workloads like making omelets or preparing delicate seafood fare – as long as it's done with wooden or plastic utensils.

If you do a lot of cooking with high heat and you're concerned about the possible health risks of non-stick cookware, or you don't want to replace your cookware every couple years, then stainless steel may be a good choice.

As a compromise, you may want to consider using stainless steel as your primary cookware while owning an inexpensive non-stick pan for delicate foods such as eggs or fish, or for preparing a quick and easy (non-stick) meal for the kids like pancakes or French toast.

Four Essential Ingredients

Just as you only need a few basic tools (out of a sea of products) to stock your kitchen, you'll find you only need to master a few simple ingredients to cook great-tasting meals at home. In fact, you'll find that just four ingredients consistently appear in recipe after recipe – the common denominator of cooking, as it were.

If you develop a basic understanding of these four key ingredients, you'll find yourself head and shoulders above your dating competition in your cooking prowess! The four ingredients are:

1. Cooking oil
2. Garlic
3. Onions
4. Salt and pepper *

*OK, salt and pepper are technically *two* ingredients, but they're so often used side by side that most of us think of them as the Yin and Yang of seasoning – inseparable both in the kitchen and on the dining room table.

Cooking Oil

The first item to get comfortable with in the kitchen is cooking oil. Cooking oil is used in cooking for two reasons – it helps prevent the food from sticking to the cookware (not as important when cooking with non-stick) and it imparts wonderful flavors to the food you're preparing.

The first step in cooking with oil is to determine what type to use. The two most common types are vegetable oil and olive oil.

Vegetable oil, like the popular Crisco and Wesson brands found in many grocery stores, is made by blending the oils from a variety of plants, nuts, fruits, and seeds. Vegetable oil comes in many varieties including canola, sunflower, soybean, and peanut oil.

Vegetable oil is the most commonly used of all the cooking oils and as such, is generally less expensive than olive oil. Because of its high smoke point – the temperature at which the oil breaks down, creating quite a bit of smoke in the process – vegetable oil is the oil of choice when high heat is needed for tasks like searing, deep frying, or popping popcorn.

Olive oil is another popular and very common cooking oil. As its name implies, it's a natural oil that's derived from the olive. Quality olive oil has a pleasant flavor and aroma that can complement many dishes. Contrary to vegetable oil, however, olive oil has a relatively low smoke point so it shouldn't be used for meals that require cooking with high heat. Olive oil also has a reputation for being the "healthy oil" since it's rich in monounsaturated fats and antioxidants and oddly enough, is the only oil that can be consumed as is, freshly pressed from the fruit.

Many cooking aficionados prefer using extra virgin olive oil whenever a recipe calls for olive oil. Extra virgin olive oil, sometimes referenced as EVOO, is a higher quality olive oil – and no, virgin doesn't mean what you might be thinking! In the context of making olive oil, the term "virgin" refers to the pressing of the olives. Extra virgin olive oil is derived from the first pressing of the olives and many say, as a result, has the most delicate flavor.

When should you use olive oil vs. vegetable oil? Ultimately, it's going to come down to personal preference. One recommendation is to use olive oil when you want a healthier alternative to vegetable oil, you desire the flavor that olive oil imparts to your food, or you're cooking with low to moderate heat. Choose a vegetable oil when you want a "cleaner" flavor, for high-heat cooking, or when you're throwing caution to the wind and simply want some greasy, comfort-food goodness!

Once you've selected the oil to use for your meal, you'll need to add the oil to the pan prior to adding the food that's to be cooked. There are two schools of thought on the best approach for adding oil to a pan. One view holds that it's better to add room temperature oil to a cold pan and then heat the pan and oil together. The logic being that you don't want to run the risk of the oil splattering up from the pan if the pan is too hot when you add the oil.

The opposing school of thought is to heat your pan first and then add the room temperature oil to the hot pan. The idea behind this approach is that the oil shouldn't be allowed to sit too long in a hot pan — the longer the oil is in contact with the hot surface of the pan, the more time there is for it to be broken down by the heat and the exposure to oxygen. Cooking oil that's heated too long gets gummy and quickly loses its flavor (and there's nothing that will kill great kitchen smells faster than the pungent odor of burning oil).

I've cooked using both approaches and quite frankly, I've not found a discernible difference in flavor between the two methods, nor have I found that room temperature oil splatters when being added to a hot pan – as long as you don't let the pan get red hot before the oil is added.

However, because I sometimes find myself getting distracted by my date or my kids while cooking, I tend to heat the pan first and then add the room temperature oil to the warm pan when I'm free of distractions. Using this approach, the risk of me leaving an unattended pan of hot oil on the stove is greatly reduced.

However, if you're working on a dish that calls for the oil to be very hot – like searing the outside of a prime filet or deep frying onion rings – then you'll want the oil sufficiently heated before you add the food to the pan. In other words, you'll want to heat the oil and pan together to ensure the oil is hot enough to sear a proper crust on the surface of the filet or properly fry your rings.

> "Searing" is a cooking term you'll see often – it's the process of briefly cooking the outside of a food item (usually a meat product) at high heat before turning the temperature down or removing the food from the heat. Searing is not intended to cook a food item thoroughly. Rather, it's used to caramelize the sugars and brown the proteins on the outside of the food – helping seal in the juices and producing a flavorful crust.

How do you know when vegetable oil is hot enough to fry onion rings or sear a steak? Ideally, the temperature of the oil should be around 350 to 375 degrees F – but that's tough to discern if you've lightly coated the bottom of a pan with oil or you have a deep pan full of oil but don't have a food thermometer handy.

If you find yourself in this predicament, you can use the wooden spoon technique. Carefully place the end of a wooden spoon in the oil and if you see bubbles forming around the wood, your oil is hot enough to cook with.

Garlic

The second ingredient to become familiar with is garlic. Garlic is a staple in the cooking world because it's easy to handle, has a long shelf life, and imparts rich flavors when added to a meal. Many recipes you come across will call for garlic cloves.

Note that a clove is not the same as a bulb – a mistake I made the first time I was cooking with garlic. A clove, as I realized later, is actually one of the little garlic pieces *inside* a bulb of garlic (a garlic bulb is what's typically sold in grocery stores). Let's just say that first meal was very well seasoned!

A bulb of garlic vs. garlic cloves

(© iStockphoto.com)

Before garlic cloves are added to your dish, you'll need to peel the thin skin from the outside of each clove. Peeling the skin from a garlic clove can be accomplished with a garlic press, and there are a myriad of garlic presses available on the market.

However, many subscribe to the less-is-more method when it comes to peeling garlic – this involves cutting off the base and tip of the clove, smashing it with the flat side of a knife (a Santoku or chef knife is ideal here but any large knife will do – be sure the sharp edge is pointed away from you), and then peeling the skin from the clove by hand.

If you're not enamored with peeling cloves, however, there's an even simpler method that does away with peeling altogether. Many grocery stores now sell bags of garlic cloves already separated from the bulb and fully peeled. If you have a bag of peeled cloves handy at home, just reach in and grab the appropriate number of cloves for the recipe you're making. It couldn't get much easier – unless the little guys cooked themselves!

Onions

The third food item to get comfortable with in the kitchen is onions. There are four types of onions that are commonly found in your local supermarket or grocery store:

1. White
2. Yellow
3. Red
4. Sweet

White onions are generally the spiciest of the onion family. Yellow onions tend to have a bit less of a "bite" than white onions. Red onions are milder than yellow onions on the "spicy" scale. And sweet onions, like the Vidalia onion found in most grocery stores, are the mildest of all four varieties.

White	Yellow	Red	Sweet
Spicy <--> Mild

The spicy to mild range for four common onions

If you only have spicy onions on hand but the recipe calls for sweet onions, you can create your own sweet onion through a process called sautéing. When an onion is sautéed, it releases a sweetened flavor. Don't let the word "sauté" scare you, however. It's just a fancy way of saying "browned."

A sautéed onion has many uses – as a key ingredient in a cooked vegetable appetizer like mushrooms and onions, as a wonderful side dish to a fine steak, or as a tasty topping on a burger.

If you've ever cooked a steak, sautéing may sound a lot like what you do when you sear a piece of meat. What's the difference between sautéing and searing? "Sauté" literally means "to jump," so when you sauté, you brown food quickly by moving (or "jumping") it around over high heat in a small amount of oil or butter – much like when stir frying. To sear is also to brown quickly over high heat – the difference is that when you sear you want to keep the food item in one place over the heat until it forms a crust on the surface.

Both techniques require high heat in order to form the caramelization on the outside of the food. Using a low heat will not meet with success – it will fail to induce the caramelization process and you may end up with food that's overcooked on the inside.

To sauté an onion you need only follow a few simple steps:

1. Heat your skillet or frying pan near high (around an 8 or 9 on a scale of 10).
2. Mince, dice, or chop the onions as called for in the recipe.
3. Add vegetable oil to the frying pan, enough to cover the bottom of the pan. Remember that olive oil has a low smoke point and is not a good choice for high-heat cooking (unless, of course, it's time to test the smoke alarms or it's "create a smelly fog in your kitchen" day).
4. Add the onions to the pan once the oil is hot (consider the wooden spoon technique), turning and stirring the

onions frequently to produce a pleasant brown exterior. Don't cover the pan, as steam will prevent the onions from browning properly.
5. Continue cooking the onions until they're evenly browned.
6. Remove from heat and serve.

And one last tip when dealing with onions. Many times you'll come across recipes that call for onions to be cut or sliced in a variety of ways – using terms like "minced," "diced," and "chopped." What's the difference? It's really quite simple – minced is the smallest cut, diced is a bit bigger, and chopped is the largest, referring to roughly ¼-inch chunks (possibly the naming committee could've made this simpler by just using "small," "medium," and "large").

From left to right – minced, diced, and chopped onions.

(© StartCooking.com at www.startcooking.com)

Salt and Pepper

The fourth and final set of cooking ingredients you should become familiar with is salt and pepper. If you enjoy the taste of salt and pepper, then you may want to indulge a bit and invest in three inexpensive cooking-related food products:

1. Sea salt
2. Peppercorn
3. A quality salt and pepper grinder set

Sea salt, which is a large-grained coarse salt as opposed to a fine-grained table salt, is obtained through the evaporation of seawater. Technically speaking, all salt is sea salt since all salt, at one point, came from the sea. Chemically, the two salts are identical (save for iodized table salt which has iodine added during the manufacturing process), and there are no proven health benefits of sea salt over table salt (though some salt manufacturers would have you believe otherwise).

From a cooking perspective the main difference between the two is not taste, but texture. Table salt is very fine and easy to dissolve while sea salt is coarser and adds a bit of "crunch" when added near the end of the meal preparation process.

Contrasted to negligible flavor differences in sea salt vs. table salt, there are pronounced differences in the flavor characteristics of peppercorn vs. table pepper. Peppercorn is just that – little corns of pepper that are cracked open at the time of use, via a grinder, to release exceptional pepper flavor and aromas. When a recipe calls for pepper, consider using cracked peppercorn instead.

> *To unlock the unique flavors of peppercorn and control the coarseness (or size) of sea salt, a grinder set is needed. I researched salt and pepper grinder sets when I moved out on my own and landed on the OXO Good Grips Salt and Pepper*

Grinder Set. The OXO Good Grips Grinder Set has several advantages.

For one, the grinders have a clear acrylic body so you'll know when it's time to add more salt or pepper. In addition, they have a precise grinding selector to change from a fine to a coarse ground product (many grinders have this feature but it often doesn't work very well), and they've yet to clog on me.

However, their best feature by far is that they're designed to rest upside down – so that the end where the grinds come out is facing up – preventing leftover grinds from making their way onto your countertop or table. You can find the reasonably priced OXO Good Grips Grinder Set online and in retail stores.

OXO Good Grips Salt and Pepper Grinder Set

(© *OXO International at* **www.oxo.com**)

Salt and Pepper to Taste

As you become more attuned to seasoning your meals, you may begin noticing the phrase "salt and pepper to taste" in many of your recipes. This simply means to add salt and pepper in whatever quantity tastes good to you – using a pinch or two (or more) of salt or a sprinkling of pepper from the grinder. There's no requirement to precisely measure the quantity used – it's all about the flavors you desire. As the saying goes, "When baking, follow directions. When cooking, go by your own taste!"

If you prefer not to add salt or pepper or your diet doesn't allow for one or the other, you can safely skip them. It won't adversely affect the outcome of the meal. By the same token, if you're cooking for a date, be careful not to add too much and risk the meal being over seasoned for her taste. Be conservative in your use of salt and pepper when cooking for a date – she can always add additional seasoning when the meal is presented to her at the table.

CHAPTER 6

Top Single Effort Recipes

In this chapter you'll find great-tasting, easy-to-make recipes for busy single guys. Besides offering terrific flavor and ease of preparation, these recipes are exceptionally versatile. They work equally well for date nights, parties, or dinner with the kids. And all are field tested and Single Effort approved!

As you consider which meals and recipes to prepare for yourself, your dates, or your kids, remember that a meal is more than the main course. You'll also need to consider a beverage to pair with your meal and a light and tasty dessert to wrap up your dining experience.

Many times the beverage served with a meal is an afterthought – decided upon at the last minute as the meal is coming out of the oven. However, keep in mind that the flavors of any meal can be heightened with a nicely paired beverage.

This could be a flavorful wine (the next chapter is devoted to discussing wine in detail and provides a simple rule of thumb for pairing wine with your meal), a great-tasting cocktail, or simply some chilled, fresh water. Whatever your drink preference, don't forget to plan a pleasing beverage to go with your meal.

As you review recipes and meal options remember not to desert the dessert. Much like a properly paired beverage, a dessert serves to complement a meal along with signaling the end of your dining experience.

Regardless of which dessert you choose to serve, be a Good Knight and don't make the portions too large. Women are always conscious of their weight and presenting your date with a large dessert portion could make her feel uncomfortable (two extremely simple-to-prepare and portion-friendly dessert recipes are covered later in this chapter).

And a final consideration that focuses on kitchen hygiene – even though there are no sacred cows in cooking there are definitely dirty cows (and no, they're not reading adult magazines – cows can't read, silly!). All animal-based food has the potential to spread food-borne illness. The best prevention is to wash your hands with soap often – before, during, and after your meal preparation. For example, after shaping ground beef into hamburger patties or removing uncooked chicken from its packaging, always wash your hands with soap before touching any other food item.

Moreover, make sure cutting boards, knives, and other utensils that come in contact with raw meat are kept away from other food items. For example, using the same knife and cutting board that was just used to cube raw chicken to also dice an onion is very dangerous. Raw chicken can be contaminated with salmonella – which could make you very ill or possibly even kill you if you ingest it. Not a great first impression if you're cooking for a date!

> Do you find yourself constantly on the go but still interested in discovering new recipes? Epicurious (**www.epicurious.com**) has an award winning kitchen companion application for smartphone and tablet users. You can search over 30,000 recipes, make interactive shopping lists, and save and share your favorite recipes – all from the comfort of your mobile device!

Sweet and Spicy BBQ Sauce

This is a top BBQ sauce recipe – containing a generous amount of both sweetness and spice. If you're looking for an easy-to-make BBQ recipe that's sure to garner delight from those that try it, look no further!

This sauce is also very versatile. It goes great with chicken, pulled pork, burgers, shrimp, or even as a mix-in with baked beans. Save any leftover sauce – it's also a great topper for green vegetables and potatoes.

Pair it with the slow cooker chicken BBQ recipe that follows and you've got an unbeatable comfort-food experience!

Total preparation time is 10 minutes once all your ingredients are *mise en place*.

<u>Ingredients</u>
- (1 ½) cups ketchup
- (1 ½) cups brown sugar
- (½) cup apple cider or red wine vinegar
- (¼) cup water
- (2 ½) tablespoons Dijon mustard
- (2) teaspoons paprika
- (2) teaspoons salt
- (2) tablespoons onion powder
- (2) teaspoons pepper
- (1) tablespoon Worcestershire sauce
- (¼) cup Italian salad dressing (Wish-Bone works well)
- A few dashes of hot pepper sauce (add more for increased heat)

Directions

Combine all the ingredients in a mixing bowl. Mix the ingredients with an electric mixer until the resulting sauce has a smooth texture.

Store in a sealed bowl and place in the refrigerator until needed.

Servings per Recipe: 20-30

Approximate Calories per Serving: 50

Fire-and-Forget Slow Cooker Chicken BBQ

This is a great "fire-and-forget" recipe for busy Dads with kids or on a date night when you want to focus on other things besides standing over the stove. It requires minimal preparation time and just about cooks itself (you don't even thaw the chicken before it's added to the cooker).

This meal goes great with just about any vegetable or as a topper to freshly cooked noodles. If you serve this meal with mashed potatoes, the leftover sauce makes an excellent gravy!

Total preparation time is 3 to 7 hours (depending on your slow cooker temperature) once all your ingredients are *mise en place*.

Ingredients

> (3 to 6) boneless, skinless chicken breasts (frozen – optional to cut these in half)
> Sweet and Spicy BBQ Sauce (preceding recipe)
> OR
> (1) 12-ounce bottle of your favorite BBQ sauce

Directions

Place the frozen chicken in the slow cooker along with the BBQ sauce. Place the cover on the slow cooker and cook for 3 to 4 hours on high or 6 to 7 hours on low.

When done, serve the chicken over freshly cooked noodles, with a vegetable, or even rolled up in a tortilla wrap with chopped lettuce and cheese – a wonderful, easy-to-make meal!

> Servings per Recipe: 4-6
> Approximate Calories per Serving: 300

Winner, Winner Creamy Chicken Dinner!

This recipe is simple to make and always gets rave reviews. The tarragon sauce in this dish takes a normal chicken dinner to an entirely new level. This recipe goes great with a side dish of green vegetables or a baked potato.

Total preparation time is about 30 minutes once you have all your ingredients *mise en place*.

Ingredients
> (2) tablespoons vegetable oil
> (1) tablespoon butter
> (4) skinless, boneless chicken breasts (thawed)
> (1) cup heavy whipping cream
> (4) teaspoons dried tarragon (also known as Dragon's Wort – cool, eh?)
> (2) tablespoons Dijon mustard

Directions

Salt and pepper the chicken breasts to taste. Heat the oil in a skillet ("skillet" is just a shorter way of saying "frying pan") over medium-high heat (around a 7 or 8 on a scale of 10).

Once the oil has come to temperature, place the chicken breasts in the skillet and brown on both sides. Reduce the heat to a bit below medium (around a 4 on a scale of 10), cover, and continue cooking for approximately 15 minutes (or until the internal temperature of the chicken reaches 165 degrees F).

> *When cooking meats like beef or poultry it's important to resist the temptation to cut the meat open to check if it's done. When you cut the meat open, you let out the juices that keep it moist and flavorful. Instead, rely on a food thermometer to accurately tell you when your meat is properly cooked.*

I've tried several food thermometers and the one I like best is the CDN ProAccurate Quick-Read Thermometer (DTQ450X). The CDN thermometer has a 5-inch stainless steel stem and the digital display is easy to read. The CDN can deliver a temperature reading in just a few seconds, and I've found it works great for all types of meat – including fish, beef, pork, and poultry.

CDN ProAccurate Quick-Read Thermometer (DTQ450X)

(© *Component Design Northwest at* **www.cdnw.com**)

Once the chicken is done, remove it from the skillet and keep it warm by placing it in a covered bowl. Keep the skillet at below medium heat (around a 4 on a scale of 10). Stir the cream into the skillet and scrape up any chicken bits that may be stuck to the bottom of the skillet (they're yummy and will be incorporated into the sauce).

Mix in the mustard and the tarragon. Continue stirring for 4 or 5 minutes or until the sauce has thickened. Return the chicken to the skillet to coat the chicken thoroughly with the sauce. Serve the chicken with a generous helping of sauce. If you've made vegetables or potatoes to go with your chicken, you can drizzle the remaining sauce over the top before serving. Delicious!

Servings per Recipe: 4

Approximate Calories per Serving: 300

Wonderfully Fresh Chicken Caesar Salad

This chicken Caesar salad recipe stands out from other Caesar salad meals because you'll be making your own croutons and salad dressing. The freshly made croutons, coupled with the warm chicken and homemade dressing, make this a wonderful (and generally healthy) salad meal. It's a terrific vegetarian meal as well – simply leave out the chicken and the anchovies.

Serve by itself or add a side dish of freshly made corn bread or lightly toasted baguette slices (a quick and easy toasted baguette recipe follows a bit later).

Total preparation time is about 25 minutes once all your ingredients are *mise en place*.

Ingredients

(2 to 3) boneless, skinless chicken breasts (thawed and sliced into bite-sized cubes)

(6) cloves garlic, 3 minced and 3 chopped (a reminder that minced is very small and chopped is chunky)

(¾) cup mayonnaise (this is one ingredient you shouldn't substitute with an alternative like Miracle Whip – the two are worlds apart from an ingredient and flavor standpoint)

(3 to 5) anchovy fillets, minced (if you're not an anchovy fan, you can skip them without significantly affecting the outcome)

(½) cup grated parmesan cheese
(¼) stick butter
(2) teaspoons Worcestershire sauce
(½) cup olive oil
(2) teaspoons Dijon mustard
(1) tablespoon lemon juice
Salt and black pepper

(4 to 5) cups bread, cubed
(1) head romaine lettuce or (2) stalks romaine hearts – torn or cut into bite-sized pieces (don't forget to wash them)

Directions

Combine the minced garlic in a small bowl with mayonnaise, anchovies, 2 tablespoons of the parmesan cheese, Worcestershire sauce, mustard, and lemon juice. Season to taste with salt and black pepper (watch the salt if you're using anchovies – they're usually quite salty on their own) and refrigerate until ready to use.

Salt the chicken cubes to taste.

Heat a large skillet over medium heat (around a 5 on a scale of 10). Add ¼ cup of the olive oil to the skillet, and then add the chicken. Cook chicken until no pink remains inside any of the chicken cubes (here it's fine to cut open a chicken cube to test for doneness as it'll be difficult to get an accurate thermometer reading from a small cube of chicken).

Turn skillet to low heat (around a 1 or 2 on a scale of 10) to keep the chicken warm.

Heat the remaining olive oil in a second skillet over medium heat (around a 5 on a scale of 10). Add the chopped garlic to the hot oil. Cook and stir until the garlic cloves are light brown, and then remove the garlic from the skillet with a wooden spoon.

Add ¼ stick of butter to the skillet and stir the oil and butter until the butter is fully melted. Then add bread cubes to the hot oil and butter mixture. Cook bread cubes, turning frequently, until lightly browned. Remove the bread cubes from the oil.

Place the bite-sized pieces of lettuce or romaine hearts in a large bowl. Toss with the warm chicken and bread cubes, dressing, and the remaining parmesan cheese. Serve while bread cubes and chicken are still warm. Sit back and enjoy – Caesar himself would be proud!

Servings per Recipe: 4-6

Approximate Calories per Serving: 450

Zesty Short Ribs

This is a fantastically flavorful short rib recipe that works equally well on date night or for dinner with the kids. It might seem counter-intuitive to boil the ribs but this helps them stay moist and juicy while allowing all the wonderful flavors of the sauce to penetrate the meat.

You can serve this meal with just about any side dish – a fresh salad, Idahoan mashed potatoes (a very easy-to-make side dish discussed a bit later), rice, and green beans are just a few examples.

Total preparation time is 80 to 90 minutes once all your ingredients are *mise en place*.

Ingredients

    (10 to 12) baby back spareribs – cut into portions (2 to 3 ribs in each portion)
    (10) cloves garlic, diced
    (½) cup soy sauce (consider the LaChoy brand of low-sodium soy sauce if you need to watch the sodium intake)
    Salt
    (1) tablespoon dried thyme
    (1) tablespoon dried oregano
    (½) of a medium-sized sweet onion, cut into quarters
    (2) tablespoons lemon juice
    (1) lime, cut into quarters

Directions

Remove the spareribs from the refrigerator and allow them to come to room temperature. Salt the meaty side of the ribs to taste.

Place the spareribs flat in a large pot and fill with just enough water to cover the top of the ribs (too much water will prolong the cooking time and cause the meat to overcook). Add the soy sauce, garlic, thyme, oregano, onion, and lemon juice to the water.

With the pot uncovered, bring the water to a boil and then adjust the heat to medium-low (around a 4 on a scale of 10) and simmer on medium-low until the water has completely evaporated. Visit the pot every 15 to 20 minutes to stir the water, turn the ribs, and ensure all the ingredients are swimming properly in the pool.

When all the water has evaporated, allow the meat to brown on the bottom of the pan, turning occasionally. Use a spatula to scrape the brown bits and softened garlic from the bottom of the pot and toss them with the ribs (giving the meat an extra kick of flavor). For even more flavor richness, consider deglazing to remove the meaty bits from the bottom of the pan.

What's "deglazing" you may ask? It's an easy (and ingenious) way to remove and enjoy the gooey bits of goodness that form on the bottom of a pan for any meal you may be preparing. Deglazing isn't complicated. It's really just a fancy word that means "pour some liquid into a very hot pan to dislodge all the bits stuck to the bottom." The liquid used for deglazing can be just about anything – from water, to broth, to heavy whipping cream or leftover wine.

The name for the resulting sauce, after those gooey bits of goodness have been deglazed, is "fond." Fond is also the French word for "bottom" (probably not the most elegant naming choice from a "Romance" language). An easy way to recall the name is to remember that you're very "fond" of the taste of those little roasted bits in their deglazed sauce (if you're not now, you will be the first time you taste them – yum!)

To deglaze a pan, remove the meat from the pan, add enough liquid to lightly coat the bottom of the pan, and turn up the heat close to high (around an 8 or 9 on a scale of 10), stirring constantly to dislodge the bits from the bottom of the pan.

You're done when all the bits have broken free of the pan and the liquid has been reduced to about half as much as when you started (or if you're using wine, until most of the alcohol in the wine has boiled off). Once done, remove the sauce, or fond, from the heat and serve it with your meal. Great with vegetables and potatoes, a fond makes a wonderful flavor bridge or can be enjoyed as a rich sauce drizzled over the main course!

The bottom of this pan is pure flavor! A little red wine with some high heat and voilà! A fond is born!

(© *Cooking for Engineers* at **www.cookingforengineers.com**)

If you're a wine enthusiast, not only does deglazing help you consume your leftover bottles of wine (red is used more often than white for deglazing), but the use of wine in the deglazing process will impart a truly unique flavor to the bits of goodness stuck to the bottom. The next time you have a bottle of wine that hasn't been fully consumed, recork the bottle and place it in your refrigerator for use in upcoming meals.

If refrigerated, an open bottle of wine that has been recorked should be fine to drink for two to three days. After that, it's not going to taste very good consumed by itself – but it'll still make for an excellent deglazing liquid for several weeks before finally succumbing to a bitter flavor.

After the bits of goodness have been removed from the bottom of the pan, place the ribs on a plate and garnish with your fond and lime wedges. Although short ribs are small in size these are definitely big on flavor – enjoy!

Servings per Recipe: 1-6

Approximate Calories per Serving: 450

Idahoan Mashed Potatoes (The Easiest Side Dish Evah!)

If you're looking for an easy-to-make side dish to go with your meal, consider picking up a package of Idahoan Mashed Potato mix. Idahoan Mashed Potatoes are probably *the* easiest side dish to make but they taste just like homemade mashed potatoes, possibly even better! Use this side dish for kids whenever you need to whip up something quickly.

Total preparation time is about 5 minutes once all your ingredients are *mise en place*.

Ingredients

(1) 4-ounce package of Idahoan Mashed Potatoes (Roasted Garlic is a favorite)
(2) cups water

Directions

Heat the water to boiling on a stovetop or in the microwave. Remove the water from the heat and carefully pour it into your serving bowl. Add the dried Idahoan Mashed Potato mix to the water and stir for 20 seconds. Done!

Servings per Recipe: 4

Approximate Calories per Serving: 110

Easy Peasy Hard-Boiled Eggs

This recipe is as much about the "show" as it is the food. Admittedly, hard-boiled eggs by themselves are usually not considered a full meal. But combined with other ingredients they can make a wonderful presentation – like in an egg salad or as a star ingredient in a pate or macaroni casserole.

Hard-boiled eggs also make a great finger food for parties or group get-togethers, including deviled eggs and Scotch eggs (eggs wrapped in sausage, rolled in breadcrumbs, and then deep-fried – does it get any better?).

The entertainment value in this recipe comes in the unique way the eggs are peeled – using the "blow" method. If you have kids, enlist their help in peeling the eggs (it's an experience they won't likely forget!).

Total preparation time is about 20 minutes once all your ingredients are *mise en place*.

Ingredients

Half dozen raw eggs (room temperature)

Directions

It's important to have your eggs at room temperature for this recipe. Place the room temperature eggs in a pot and fill the pot with water until there's approximately 2 inches of water above the top of the eggs.

Place the pot on the stove and heat the water to a boil using high heat (around an 8 on a scale of 10). Once the water is boiling, turn the heat to medium (around a 5 on a scale of 10) and start a timer to allow the eggs to cook for 7 minutes.

After you've started the timer, grab a medium-sized bowl and fill it 2/3 full with cold water. Add a full tray of ice cubes to the bowl of cold water.

Once the eggs have hit the 7-minute mark, turn off the heat and remove the eggs, one at a time, from the hot water with a slotted spoon – placing each egg gingerly in the bowl of ice water (a slotted spoon is used to prevent the transfer of the hot water into the ice water).

Allow the eggs to sit in the ice water for 5 minutes. After the 5 minutes are up, drain the ice and water from the bowl. Your eggs are now perfectly cooked.

To peel your eggs, crack each end of the egg and remove a small ring of shell from it (approximately ½ inch in diameter). Now grasp the egg in your hands and blow through one of the open ends of the shell. When you blow hard enough the egg will pop from its shell and into your hands.

Run the egg under cold water to remove any leftover shell fragments and *voilà*! A fully peeled hard-boiled egg! Easy Peasy!

Servings per Recipe: 6

Approximate Calories per Serving: 85

A Side of Toasted Baguette Slices

Toasted baguette slices make for a terrific side dish – they pair well with just about any meal, taste delicious, and they're simple to make. Not only can you serve baguette slices as part of your meal but they also make a great finger food for parties.

Total preparation time is about 15 minutes once all your ingredients are *mise en place*.

Ingredients

(1) French baguette (most grocery stores sell them – make sure it's fresh)
(¼) cup olive oil
Fresh ground pepper (optional)
(1) clove garlic, minced (optional)
(1) jar of oil-packed sun-dried tomatoes (optional)

Directions

If you're using a traditional oven, remove any unused pans from the oven and pre-heat the broiler to high. If you're using a toaster oven, there should be no need to pre-heat unless the manufacturer's instructions call for it.

Slice your baguette bread into ¼-inch thick slices and place the bread on a pizza pan.

If you don't have a pizza pan handy, you can use the slotted top of a broiler pan. If nothing else is available, a cookie sheet will do in a pinch.

> If you haven't used a pizza pan to make pizza or toasted bread, consider giving it a try. The secret to a pizza pan's knack for turning out great pizza and toasted bread is its perforated design. The perforations in the pan allow the heat to infuse through the bottom of the dough – resulting in a pleasantly crisp bottom crust.

Brush the tops of the baguette slices lightly with olive oil using a pastry brush. If you don't have a pastry brush, simply pour the olive oil into a small bowl and gingerly dip the tops of the bread into the oil. If you want to spice things up a bit you can add fresh ground pepper or minced garlic to the tops of the baguettes after the oil has been applied. Oil-packed sun-dried tomatoes work great as a baguette topper, too!

Once the olive oil and any other toppings have been applied, place the bread in the oven on the middle rack and broil or toast the baguette slices for 5 to 7 minutes or until the bread is lightly browned. Keep a watchful eye on the bread – it doesn't take much for it to go from a pleasing light brown to a burnt, crispy critter! Remove the baguettes from the oven and serve warm. Simple and scrumptious!

Servings per Recipe: 8-10

Approximate Calories per Serving: 100

Mini Graham Cracker Jell-O Pudding Pie Dessert

Every good meal should end with a great dessert. If you cook a stellar dinner but your dessert falls flat, your date may not remember the stellar dinner – only that your dessert left a lot to be desired.

A great dessert doesn't have to be complicated or time consuming to prepare. For a no-bake dessert that's sure to please and easy for any single guy to make at home, this recipe takes the proverbial cake!

Total preparation time is about 15 minutes once all your ingredients are *mise en place*.

Ingredients

(1) package of Keebler Ready Crust Mini Graham Cracker Pie Crusts (found in most grocery stores)

(1) 3.9-ounce package of Jell-O Instant Pudding and Pie Filling (there are many flavors to choose from – chocolate, vanilla, and banana cream are three favorites)

(1) 8-ounce tub of Cool Whip

(2) cups cold milk (consider using low fat if you or your date are counting calories)

(1) 8-ounce package of Nestle chocolate chip morsels (optional)

(1) Hershey's milk chocolate bar (optional)

Directions

Mix the Jell-O pudding with the milk according to the package directions. After the pudding has been mixed, place it in the refrigerator for approximately 5 minutes to thicken just a bit (this makes it easier to scoop the pudding from the bowl in the next step).

After the 5 minutes are up, remove the pudding from the refrigerator and scoop it into the Keebler pie crusts. Cover the filled pie crusts and place them in the refrigerator.

When it's time to serve the pudding pies, remove them from the refrigerator and place a healthy scoop of Cool Whip on top of each pie.

For an added touch of flair, use a small grater to flake a bit of the Hershey's bar on top of the Cool Whip or delicately place a few Nestle morsels on top of each pie and serve. Delicious!

Servings per Recipe: 6

Approximate Calories per Serving: 250

Creamy Fruit Dip (Aka Foolproof Dessert)

This dessert recipe is about as easy and foolproof as it gets from an ingredient and preparation standpoint – yet it tastes amazing! You can use this recipe for dessert on date nights or as a fun sweet treat to make and enjoy with your kids.

It's a fantastic dessert to take to dinner parties due to its portability and ease of setup, and it also makes for a great fruit salad topping!

Total preparation time is about 10 minutes once all your ingredients are *mise en place*.

Ingredients

(1) 8-ounce package of Kraft Philadelphia brand cream cheese

(1) 7-ounce jar of marshmallow creme (Jet-Puffed works very well)

(1) teaspoon vanilla extract

(1) slice fresh pineapple, cut into cubes

(2 to 4) cups fresh strawberries

Directions

Ensure the cream cheese is at room temperature and softened by removing it from the refrigerator about 30 to 45 minutes before it's to be used.

The marshmallow creme can be a bit difficult to get out of its jar without making a sticky mess everywhere. To lessen the chance of gummy mayhem, apply a light coat of olive oil to a rubber spatula and use the oil-coated spatula to remove the marshmallow creme from the jar. The creme will be less likely to stick to the oil-coated spatula – reducing the odds that you'll end up with marshmallow creme residue all over the spatula, your hands, and the kitchen counter.

Combine the cream cheese, vanilla extract, and marshmallow creme. Use an electric mixer to blend the ingredients together into a creamy mixture.

Once the dip is mixed well, add the pineapple cubes into the dip and blend again with the mixer until the cubes have been broken down and fully incorporated into the dip (very few lumps). Store the dip in the refrigerator until ready to serve.

Serve on top of a fresh fruit salad or as a great-tasting dip for fresh strawberries. Dunk the strawberries into the fruit dip and eat – repeat until full!

Servings per Recipe: 4-6

Approximate Calories per Serving: 150

CHAPTER 7

"Wining" for All the Right Reasons

Learning the basics of cooking is a great first step into the world of the culinary arts but it's only half the equation when it comes to serving an enticing meal. As touched upon in the last chapter, a beverage, like a good wine, paired properly with a meal can enhance the entire dining experience.

As with men who know how to cook, many women are also impressed by a guy who understands wine. It shows you have a degree of sophistication, that you're a bit more "worldly" than their average date or guy friend. However, don't think of wine as just a "date thing" or something that needs to be served with a meal. A nice glass of wine can be enjoyed alone with a good book or can complement a relaxing movie night at home.

Are you a non-drinker or possibly don't care for wine? No problem-o! You can still impress women with your wine knowledge – even if you don't imbibe. With just a little wine know-how you can rest easy ordering a proper wine for your date (assuming, of course, that she's a wine drinker).

Women unfamiliar with wine or not knowledgeable enough to feel comfortable ordering wine on their own will appreciate a Good Knight who can confidently pair a nice bottle of wine with a meal. If your date seems interested in a glass of wine but is struggling to decide, impress her with your wine knowledge by assisting with her selection.

Wine was always a mystery to me when I was married. It seemed too complicated and "sophisticated" to understand. Cabernet Sauvignon? Riesling? What the heck *were* these names? There were so many varieties of wine, with just as many strange-sounding monikers – how could anyone make sense of it all?

When I became single, I decided to pull the stop chain on the ignorance bus and learn about wines and the winemaking process. After a bit of study I no longer feel intimidated discussing wine with friends or ordering a bottle of wine on a dinner date. And if *I* can learn about wine – someone who didn't know a cork pull from a cork board – anyone can!

In this chapter the veil of secrecy will be lifted and you'll gain the confidence you need to order wine on a date, talk intelligently about wine in a social setting, and start enjoying the wonderful world of wining – for all the right reasons!

Two Simple Facts About Wine

With literally thousands of wines on the market, choosing a bottle can seem like a daunting task – but it's really quite simple once you understand two facts about wine that every single guy should know.

Simple Fact #1: Wine Equals Grapes
Wine is simply juice from mashed-up grapes. That's it – nothing more. Wine equals grapes.

Now that you realize wine is merely squashed grapes, the next part will be easy to understand. You know those fancy wine names you've seen in restaurants and stores – like Cabernet Sauvignon, Pinot Noir, and Chardonnay? Well, they're simply the names of the particular grape variety used to make the wine.

The name of a wine is usually derived from the type of grape (or grapes) used to make it – simple, eh?

Simple Fact #2: Wine Is Not Beer
Unfortunately (or fortunately – depending on your point of view) wine is not like beer, soda, liquor, or even water. Every bottle of wine is different. This uniqueness is due to the distinct characteristics of the grapes that make up the wine and to the winemaking process.

All the variables of winemaking coalesce in the fact that wine from the same vineyard will end up tasting slightly different from one aging barrel to another, let alone wine from entirely different vineyards.

Kicking it old school, consider ordering a Pabst Blue Ribbon while visiting France (there's got to be a producer over there somewhere) and later Detroit – they'll both taste very similar if not exactly the same. In fact, regardless of where they're produced, they're *supposed* to taste the same.

However, if you order a glass of Cabernet Sauvignon from the Bordeaux region of France, even though it shares the same name – "Cabernet Sauvignon" – as one from the Napa Valley of California, it *will* taste different. This uniqueness is at the heart of what makes wine enjoyable and interesting.

The uniqueness of wine can be compared to walking through a Costco or Sam's Club. It's never 100% the same each time – there's always something new to see, taste, and explore. As you get to know the ins and outs of wine you'll come to see that wine is a lot like strolling the aisles of your local warehouse club. The "Costco Effect"!

Congratulations! You now know more about wine than most guys, single or not. But keep reading – there's still more to discover…

Red and White Demystified (When Purple = Red)

The grape variety used to make a wine is the single most important factor in winemaking and determines what type of wine will be made. Most wines are made from either red or white grapes. A red wine is made from red grapes and a white wine is made from white grapes. However, someone long ago took great liberty in describing the color of winemaking grapes. A "red" grape is actually much more purple in color than red and a "white" grape is actually green.

Popular red wines (remember, red wines are made from purple…err…red grapes) that you may come across are

Cabernet Sauvignon, Merlot, Syrah or Shiraz, Pinot Noir, and Zinfandel. Popular white wines (from green – aka white – grapes) include Chardonnay, Riesling, Sauvignon Blanc, and Pinot Grigio.

A not-often-discussed aspect of winemaking grapes is that under their skin, the color of a white grape is actually the same as that of a red grape. Thus Zinfandel (a common *red* wine) and White Zinfandel (an obvious *white* wine) are actually made from the same grapes – in the case of White Zinfandel, minus the skins.

Besides their color, there are two other important distinctions between red and white wines. The first distinction is that white wine doesn't generally benefit from aging and can be consumed shortly after bottling. Red wine, on the other hand, *does* benefit – its flavor is enhanced as the wine continues to age in its bottle. The other important distinction is that white wine is generally served chilled while red wine is not.

Regardless of whether you plan to select a red or a white wine, you may be asking, "With so many wines on the market, how do I choose a good bottle of wine for my evening date?" or "Exactly what is the definition of a *good* wine?"

Unfortunately, there isn't a hard-and-fast rule. What tastes good to one person may not resonate with someone else – it's all a matter of personal preference. It's up to you to make a habit of visiting wines often – tasting and experimenting in order to find the wines you enjoy. The Costco Effect in action!

Alexis Lichine, a famous Russian wine author and entrepreneur, said it best – "When it comes to wine, I tell people to throw away the vintage charts and invest in a corkscrew. The best way to learn about wine is the drinking."

If you're fortunate enough to live near a winery, consider a Single Effort date night for some wine tasting. You'll have a great time sampling many of your locally grown wines with your date and getting to know her while at the same time learning more about wine and the winemaking process.

Six Types of Wine Reviewed

To help you get a feel for the wine landscape and the many choices you have when selecting a good wine, let's look at six of the most popular wines – three red and three white.

The red wines reviewed here include:
- Cabernet Sauvignon
- Pinot Noir
- Zinfandel

The white wines reviewed here include:
- Sauvignon Blanc
- Chardonnay
- Riesling

Lace up your wining moccasins and spend a few minutes walking the Single Effort vineyards – you'll learn all you need to know to order with confidence and enjoy several popular red and white wines!

Cabernet Sauvignon (Red Wine)

Cabernet Sauvignon is one of the world's most widely recognized red grape varieties. Cabernet Sauvignon grapes are grown all over the globe – in nearly every major wine-producing country. Many people refer to Cabernet Sauvignon as the king of red grapes. This may be due to the fact that the grape can be grown in a number of climates and produces a wine with a wide range of flavor characteristics.

Cabernet Sauvignon grapes

(© Napa Valley Vintners at www.napavintners.com)

The Cabernet Sauvignon grape is a small berry with a thick skin, giving it a high solid to juice ratio and creating a wine high in color and tannin. What's a "tannin" you may ask? Tannins are very important in the winemaking process. They give a wine color, structure, and a bit of flavor. Tannins are often described as "puckery" or bitter in taste and said to leave a drying sensation in the mouth – akin to licking a cotton ball.

Because the Cabernet Sauvignon grape adapts to so many different soils and climates and can flourish with different types of winemaking, its characteristics vary depending on its origin. In the French Bordeaux you'll find more of the earthy, tannic side of Cabernet. In warmer regions like California and Australia, you'll frequently get more ripe fruit flavors up front.

Cabernet Sauvignon grapes are picked when higher in fruit and lower in acid, often producing a more "approachable" wine – this is a great first wine for someone who's new to the wine experience. If you're on a date and not sure what red wine to order, try a bottle of Cabernet Sauvignon. It's a fantastic first step into the world of wine.

Common descriptors used to convey the flavor and smell characteristics of Cabernet Sauvignon include black currant, herbs, cedar, vanilla, tobacco, mint, sweet wood, and earthy.

Pinot Noir (Red Wine)

The name Pinot Noir is derived from the French words *pinot*, meaning "pine," and *noir*, meaning "black." Although Pinot Noir grapes are now grown around the world, mostly in the cooler regions, they hail from the Burgundy region of France and are still chiefly grown there.

Pinot Noir is a finicky grape. It only grows in the right climate, with the right soils and the right care. Perhaps the fact that the grape is so difficult to grow is what makes the wine so loved. Pinot Noir grapes are widely considered to produce some of the finest wines in the world.

A great inspiration for learning about wine (and laughing at wine culture) is the 2004 movie *Sideways*. The film is a lighthearted look at two men in their forties, one divorced and one about to be married (ironically, given the context), on a road trip through California wine country. It made quite a splash when it was released and is credited with increasing U.S. and British sales of Pinot Noir – the wine favored by one of the film's main characters – and with drawing traffic to California's Santa Ynez Valley where the story takes place.

Pinot Noir grapes

(© *Napa Valley Vintners at* **www.napavintners.com**)

Pinot Noir grapes are also used in the production of champagne and sparkling wines. Did you ever wonder what the difference was between sparkling wine and champagne? The answer, in most cases, is nothing – just the name is different. It turns out the French are very fussy about the use of the word "champagne." Only sparkling white wine that comes from the Champagne region of France can be called champagne.

In fact, it's been a law in Europe since the late 1800s that only Champagne vineyards can call their wine champagne. In America, however, it's perfectly legal to call your sparkling wine "champagne," but most American wine producers continue to respect the French tradition in labeling their products.

Common flavor descriptors for Pinot Noir include aromas of red fruit, summer pudding, and baking spices.

Zinfandel (Red Wine)

Zinfandel is another popular red wine, brought to the United States in the early 1800s. Today, California is a top producer of Zinfandel and it competes with Cabernet Sauvignon as California's most popular red wine. Zinfandel is also grown in other states one might not expect including Colorado, Illinois, Ohio, Oregon, and Texas.

Zinfandel grapes

(© ShutterStock at www.shutterstock.com)

Because Zinfandel grapes often have higher levels of sugar than other comparable red wine grapes, Zinfandel grapes can produce wines with higher levels of alcohol and bursting, fruity flavors.

Common flavor descriptors for Zinfandel include robust, fruity, raspberry, raisins, blackberry, and "jam-like."

Sauvignon Blanc (White Wine)

Sauvignon Blanc grapes get their name from the French words *sauvage*, meaning "wild," and *blanc*, meaning "white."

Originating in the Loire Valley of France, this grape is now grown all around the world – in places like California, New Zealand, South Africa, and Brazil.

Sauvignon Blanc grapes

(© *Napa Valley Vintners at* **www.napavintners.com**)

Depending on the climate in which the grapes are grown, Sauvignon Blanc's wine flavor can range from grassy to tropical. Sauvignon Blanc is a very versatile white wine that can be paired nicely with a range of foods – from a chicken Caesar salad to a white-sauce pasta dish or a vegetarian meal.

Common flavor descriptors used to characterize a Sauvignon Blanc include crisp, grassy, lemon, lime, passion fruit, elegant, green apple, and fresh.

Chardonnay (White Wine)
Similar to Cabernet Sauvignon, the Chardonnay grape is a fairly low-maintenance variety that has adapted to a variety of climates. Chardonnay hails from the vineyards of Burgundy,

France, but is now grown across the United States, South Africa, Australia, and New Zealand.

Chardonnay grapes

(© *Napa Valley Vintners at* **www.napavintners.com**)

Chardonnay is generally considered a "dry" wine. How can a beverage, liquid by definition, be dry? It's all about the sweetness. The less sweet tasting the wine the "drier" it is considered. Most table wines (wines that you would serve with a meal) are considered dry wines.

The classic martini is made by adding vermouth (considered a sweet wine) to gin. When you order a dry martini the bartender simply puts less vermouth in the drink to make it less sweet, or more "dry." Shaken or stirred – wine makes a great addition to many popular cocktails!

Chardonnay is one of America's top-selling white wines. Because of the high volume of Chardonnay sold in the United States, a wide variety of low-cost Chardonnay wines are available for purchase. Some very good Chardonnays can be had for under $15 a bottle.

Common flavor descriptors for Chardonnay include oak, citrus, pear, and tropical fruit.

Riesling (White Wine)

Riesling is a white grape variety that originated in the Rhine region of Germany and is now grown all over the world – in places like Washington State, New York State, Austria, France, and South Africa. Riesling grapes are best grown in a cooler climate.

Riesling grapes

(© ShutterStock at www.shutterstock.com)

A Riesling's flavor is usually characterized as sweet (but it can actually vary from extremely dry to very sweet). Riesling wine usually has a high level of acidity but that's offset by its floral and fruit aromas. Like Sauvignon Blanc, Riesling is a very versatile wine. If you're ever at a loss for which white wine to pair with your meal, a Riesling is a great choice.

Common flavor descriptors for Riesling wines include peach, mineral, steely, citrus, sweet, and floral.

Where to Find Great Wine

Now that you know more about wine than most guys, you're probably anxious to go out and buy a bottle or two. That's great! If this is your first time buying a bottle of wine and you need help selecting the right wine for your evening or event, you may want to consider visiting your local wine store and having them suggest a nice $20 bottle of Cabernet Sauvignon (red wine) or a Riesling (white wine). Twenty dollars should get you a very good bottle of wine and you'll be off to the races!

If $20 is a bit steep and you're lucky enough to have a Trader Joe's (**www.traderjoes.com**) near you, the Charles Shaw brand of wines is an excellent value at only $2.99 a bottle (at the time of this book's publishing). Several years ago these wines were introduced exclusively at Trader Joe's at a price of $1.99 a bottle, earning them the nickname "Two Buck Chuck." The Charles Shaw brand proves the adage that high quality doesn't necessarily have to come at a high price.

And finally, don't forget Consumer Reports (they produce excellent wine lists based on consumer feedback and in-house reviews) and the Internet – with top sites like the Wine Spectator (**www.winespectator.com**) and Decanter.com (**www.decanter.com**).

Storing Your Wine for Maximum Flavor

Once you've done your shopping and have your wine bottles in tow, you'll need to store them properly to ensure they stay flavorful until opened. Unfortunately, you can't store wine the same way you'd store a soda or a beer (how great would that be – a wine six pack!). However, the rules for storing wine are not complicated.

A couple key points you need to know about storing your wine:

DO pay attention to temperature. Around 55 degrees F is ideal for storing wine, but average room temperatures of 68 to 70 degrees F are fine as well. The most important thing is to make sure the temperature remains fairly constant. It's better to store wine in a room where you have a constant 70 degrees F than one where the temperature is continually fluctuating from 60 to 70 degrees F.

DON'T store your wine in bright light. The darker the storage area for wine the better. Bright light can damage the flavor of a wine (hence the invention of the wine cellar – it really does have a purpose). This could be as simple as storing your wine in a closet or utilizing a dark corner of the basement or an unused cupboard.

DON'T store your wine bottles where they're susceptible to vibration. For example, storing your wine on top of the refrigerator or the clothes washer is probably not a good idea (let alone inside the washer – which, although a dark location, is not going to be met with much success). Also, if you're chilling your wine, don't place it in the refrigerator door where it'll be susceptible to vibrations from the door opening and closing.

DO keep the cork in the wine bottle wet. This is why an enterprising person, long ago, invented the wine rack – so that the wine bottle can sit horizontally to keep the wine in contact with the cork and prevent the cork from drying out. Dry corks contract, allowing air into the bottle. Unfortunately, when air enters a bottle many of the wine's great flavors escape. Some wineries have moved to a synthetic cork to alleviate the problem of traditional corks drying out. If you have wine with a synthetic cork you can safely store it upright. If you're unsure what type of cork your wine bottle uses, play it safe and store your wine horizontally.

Fare Thee Well, Wine. How Do I Serve Thee?

As mentioned earlier, when serving your wine there's a simple rule to remember – white wines should be chilled before serving and red wines should be served at room temperature. This isn't done for snobbish reasons. A properly chilled bottle of white wine, just like a cold can of beer, does indeed taste better than a room temperature bottle of white wine. While there's certainly no harm in chilling red wine – indeed, some people prefer their red wine chilled – based on convention and common practice, it's usually the white wine that gets chilled before serving.

For white wine, a couple hours in the refrigerator is sufficient. Then, 20 to 30 minutes before serving, remove the wine from the refrigerator (you want to serve it chilled but not cold – serving white wine cold will mask many of its flavors). If you've forgotten to put your white wine in the refrigerator before serving you can use a small bucket filled with ice water to quickly chill your wine before it's to be served.

Prior to serving your wine – red or white – you're obviously going to need to remove the cork. You'll find a startling assortment of devices on the market whose sole purpose in life is to extract the cork from a bottle of wine. Getting at the contents of a wine bottle is a simple concept that has generated hundreds of different designs.

After going through several brands of wine openers I finally landed on what should be the last cork pull you'll ever need. It's called the OXO Steel CorkPull Wine Opener (as you've probably already surmised, I'm a fan of the OXO brand – their products do what they say they'll do, without compromise).

The OXO cork pull performs its magic by using a hand-operated, screw-powered design that makes removing the cork from the bottle almost effortless.

The OXO Steel CorkPull is a very solid and well-thought-out device in a compact form (so it stores easily when not in use). Besides being a great cork pull, it also contains a built-in foil cutter for gaining access to the cork if it's sealed in foil.

There are other more expensive (and quite a few less expensive) wine openers on the market – but none that work as effortlessly as the OXO Steel CorkPull in such a small package. For a single guy to use in his home, the OXO Steel CorkPull Wine Opener gets the Single Effort wine seal of approval!

The OXO Steel CorkPull Wine Opener

*(© OXO International at **www.oxo.com**)*

Pairing Your Wine with Food

You now understand the principal elements of wine and how it's made, you know how best to store your wine, and you're also clear on how to serve your wine – you're well on your way to becoming a wine connoisseur!

However, before you uncork that perfect bottle of wine, make sure you've selected the right wine for the occasion.

If you're drinking wine by itself, the wine you choose will simply depend on your mood and the flavor requirements you have at the moment. However, if you're drinking wine with a meal, take a minute to ensure you've paired the wine properly with the food you intend to serve (or are being served).

Can't or don't want to remember what wine to use when – but still interested in pairing wine properly when eating out? Enlist the help of a sommelier. Sommelier (pronounced "som mil yay") is a French word that means "wine steward." This is the person in charge of wines and wine service at a restaurant. Their goal is to make sure customers are happy with their wine selection by suggesting wines that will best complement your meal.

Pairing the right wine with your food will heighten the taste of your meal and contribute to the success of your evening. Unfortunately, there are many complicated and contrasting "rules" and opinions when it comes to pairing wine with food – everyone's an expert, it seems.

While most of us are *not* wine experts, we *do* know simple and easy-to-remember when we see it. The Single Effort rule of thumb for pairing wine with food is straightforward and should serve you well in almost all situations:

Pair white wine with white foods and red wine with red foods.

Here are several examples:

Food Type	Red Wine	White Wine
Fish		X
Red Meats	X	
White Meats		X
Casseroles and Stews	X	
Pasta (Red Sauces)	X	
Pasta (White Sauces)		X
Vegetarian	X	X
Marshmallows		X
Red Velvet Cake	X	

Wine pairing examples for common food categories

OK – the last two examples might be a bit of a reach. Keep reading, however – you're in the home stretch!

> If you'd like to continue your journey through the vineyards and learn more about wine and winemaking, I'd recommend the book *Wine for Dummies* by Ed McCarthy and Mary Ewing-Mulligan.

Pairing the right wine with your dinner will definitely enhance the meal and contribute to the success of your evening. Wine (in moderation!) is also known for creating a relaxed mood that lets a man's best self shine through. Indeed, as the late English author Samuel Johnson once said, "Wine gives a man nothing – it only puts in motion what had been locked up in frost."

Remember to give yourself time to defrost a little every now and then. Uncork a bottle of your favorite wine and bring out what might have been locked up for years. Women are impressed by a man who understands wine – for all the right reasons!

CHAPTER 8

Meeting New Women – Stack the Odds in Your Favor!

Once you've had time to establish yourself in your home and you've brushed up on your cooking and wine skills, you may want to consider meeting new women. Outstanding – and exciting! But the age-old question remains: where do you go to meet them?

Most guys, at one time or another, have answered that question by trying to meet new women at bars and nightclubs. Sometimes this approach can meet with success but often, it does not. It can be difficult to talk to a woman you've just met in a noisy bar or club – and your odds of finding Ms. Right are lessened further by the fact that, in these settings, men generally outnumber women by a significant margin.

In addition, trying to meet new people in a large group setting can place you at a disadvantage. According to a study published in the journal *Psychological Science,* people are more likely to rely on physical characteristics, such as height or weight, to make their dating choice in larger groups (as physical characteristics don't take much time to review and assess) than on characteristics that require "getting to know you" time

– like occupational status or education (see "How Humans Cognitively Manage an Abundance of Mate Options" by Alison P. Lenton and Marco Francesconi at **pss.sagepub.com/content/21/4/528.full**).

What this study implies is that when women view you within a large group of other guys, they're going to rely on your physical characteristics more than your intellect or charm. This is perhaps borne out by a famous quote from Mary Poppins (for the uninitiated, *Mary Poppins* appears to be required viewing for all young girls, who usually insist their dads watch, too – over, and over, and over): "Though we adore men individually, we agree that as a group they're rather stupid."

Of course, none of us are stupid (though we've probably found ourselves near the front of the pack from time to time) but we do need to be aware of the lens through which we're being viewed – especially in large groups.

Where to Meet Women

Because most of us aren't blessed with the physical attributes of a young Arnold Schwarzenegger or a dashing Brad Pitt, it behooves us to put ourselves in situations where we can leverage our physical attributes *and* our non-physical characteristics – like intelligence, wit, humor, and charm – in attracting new women.

Instead of trying to meet new women in a large group setting packed with your competition or in the same well-worn locations that every other guy is using, stack the odds in your favor by seeking out more creative and unique places to make new acquaintances. Places where the women generally outnumber the men and where you can shine individually with both your physical and non-physical attributes.

In this chapter you'll find unique Single Effort suggestions for where you can meet new women and shine as a distinct and individual guy. In fact, in some of these places, the odds will *very* much be in your favor – you'll be the only guy around!

Single Effort suggestions for where to meet new women include:

- Foraging for food
- Joining a fitness class
- Volunteering your time
- Learning how to dance
- Joining an association or organization
- Enrolling in an adult education class
- Shopping in a women's clothing or personal care store

One note of caution, however – be sure that whatever activity or location you choose, you do so because you want to be there and have a genuine interest in the activity. Don't do it simply because you like the dating prospects. Women will be able to tell if your interest is simply for "pick-up" purposes, and you'll likely come across as shallow and insincere.

Where? Foraging for Food

We all need to eat and therefore, we all must eventually go foraging for food. Unless you hunt and kill your own food, this usually means a trip to the grocery store. Take advantage of everyone's eventual need for food! Single Effort your grocery shopping by meeting new women at the same time.

As mentioned earlier, grocery stores are usually "ripe" with single women, especially during the evening hours. And there's a definite advantage to meeting women in a grocery store – when you strike up a conversation with a woman there, you'll have the benefit of gaining insight into her world (and discovering topics to bring up when opening a conversation with her) simply by observing what's in her grocery cart.

Do you see lots of vegetables but no meat products in her cart? She could be a vegetarian. Is she pushing around several cans of baby food? Most likely she has a small child to care for. Does she have a bag of dog or cat food in her cart? She could be a pet lover.

Key in on the items you see in her cart as possible points of entry into a conversation (if you're not sure how to approach a woman or don't know what to say, don't worry – the next chapter's got you covered!).

For example, if you see cat treats in her cart bring up a discussion about kittens. If you see wine, leverage your wine knowledge and discuss the merits of white vs. red. Take advantage of the small insight you have into her world to create a dialogue that will interest her (and don't forget that the Grocery Cart Effect is in your corner as well!).

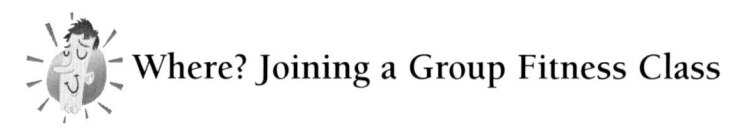

Where? Joining a Group Fitness Class

In addition to eating, we all need to practice healthy living and keep ourselves in shape. Single Effort taking care of your health and well-being and meeting new women by joining a group fitness class. If you meet someone you like in your class, you'll already have a great idea of what she looks like in her natural element (i.e. little to no makeup and everyday clothes). You'll also have the benefit of knowing she's serious about keeping herself in shape and she'll know that about you as well.

I've attended many group aerobics classes and average attendance is usually around 90% women and 10% men. Many times, I was the only guy in the class. Not bad odds!

If you're not into aerobics you may want to consider taking a yoga or Pilates class. Not only are yoga and Pilates classes a great way to stay in shape (they're tougher than they look), but most are still (incorrectly) considered by many men to be "female-only" activities. As a result, these classes are generally well populated with women.

Keep in mind that not only is staying in shape healthy and better for your well-being, it also pays dividends by allowing you to cast a wider net when dating. Your pool of dating candidates *will* be larger if you're in good shape than if you're not.

Yes, people shouldn't judge others by their looks but we all do it. Unfortunately, it's the world we live in (don't despair, tips on grooming and how to dress and look your best are right around the corner in the chapter 9). If you're not already, start eating right and exercising more to ensure you're swimming in the biggest dating pool possible.

Where? Volunteering Your Time

Many times we get so caught up in ourselves that it's easy to forget those less fortunate. Single Effort helping those in need while meeting women who share your caring for others by volunteering your time.

After becoming single I realized that most of my life had been devoted to "me" things with very little of my time spent giving back to others in the community. I decided to change that and began volunteering at a local homeless shelter. I took my kids to the shelter with me and we prepared, cooked, and served dinner for the residents. I found that volunteering at the local shelter was also a great way to meet new people, as there was always a constant flow of new volunteers.

If you have kids and they're allowed to join you when you volunteer, consider taking them with you – it'll be an invaluable experience for them. Helping those in need puts kids in touch with what's important in life, giving them a perspective they might not otherwise get, showing them the importance of community, and helping them realize that nothing should ever be taken for granted.

Where? Learning How to Dance

One of the few things that *can* be taken for granted however is that most women like to dance. And yet, in what can only be seen as a cruel irony, most guys would probably not count dancing as one of the top 50 things they'd like to do on a date.

Why not learn a skill that you know most women will appreciate and that most of your dating competition is probably not very good at? Single Effort meeting new women and learning a talent that will pay back dividends in all your relationships by enrolling in dance lessons (dancing is a great way to stay in shape, too!).

Most likely, several dance schools in your area teach the basics of dance. Many community colleges and your local community events calendar will typically advertise dance lessons as well.

As the poet Robert Frost once said, "Dancing is a vertical expression of a horizontal desire." If that isn't reason enough to learn how to dance, I don't know what is!

Where? Joining an Organization

Another great way to meet women and make new friends is by participating in professional organizations and associations. Single Effort meeting new women and learning a new skill or building on an existing talent by joining an organization or association (the terms "association" and "organization" are, for all intents and purposes, one and the same). There are thousands of professional organizations and associations available to join depending on your interests.

But here again the sincerity rule comes into play. When seeking out an organization to join, be sure to find one that fits your interests – don't just join because you like the dating prospects. Members will be able to sense if your participation isn't sincere and you're only there for the dating opportunities. Fake interest is rarely charming!

> Not sure where to find a professional association that might interest you? A great place to start is Wikipedia (**www.wikipedia.org**). You can find a list of over 400 professional associations on the Wikipedia site at **www.en.wikipedia.org/wiki/Category:Professional_associations**.

After my divorce, as a way to meet new people and broaden my horizons, I joined the Toastmasters International organization (**www.toastmasters.org**). Though perhaps ill-named (no toasted bread involved, in case you're wondering), Toastmasters is an organization with a worthy purpose – to help people develop their public speaking and leadership skills – and it's well known in the business community.

I've met many wonderful people through Toastmasters (none that I've dated but a few that will likely be lifelong friends) and at the same time improved my public speaking skills – something I hope to use and carry with me for the rest of my life.

Where? Enrolling in a Class

When you become single again you'll most likely find that you have more time to yourself than you did when you were married or in a relationship. Consider putting that time to good use by pursuing a skill or passion you've always wanted to develop. Single Effort meeting new women and developing a creative passion by enrolling in an adult education class.

If possible, try to focus on classes that you feel will contain a high percentage of single women. Recommendations include classes in the arts like pottery, painting, photography, music, or drawing. You can also sign up for more practical courses like cooking, self-defense, or CPR. Take advantage of the additional time you may now have on your hands to join a class, learn a new skill, and meet new women at the same time.

There's a flip side here as well. For every class that's offered there are two categories of people that must attend: the student and the teacher. Most of us would probably assume that we fall into the "student" category – but many times that undervalues our talents.

If you have a skill you think others would be interested in, offer up your services to teach at a local community college or in a continuing education class. This is a great way to Single Effort meeting new women while developing your teaching and speaking skills and helping others learn a new talent.

You don't have to be a certified teacher or an expert in a particular field to teach, either. All of us have something we know or do well that we could teach others.

Maybe you know how to make killer muffins and pastries and would enjoy teaching the basics of baking at your local community center. Perhaps you've got a green thumb and would enjoy educating others on how to take care of their plants and flowers. Maybe you're a natural with computers and would like to pass along your tech knowledge. Whatever skills you have, look into sharing your knowledge with others while meeting new women – Single Effort style!

Where? Shopping in a Women's Store

Do you have a mother, sister, daughter, or niece who's going to need a gift for an upcoming birthday or holiday? Women's clothing and personal care stores (fragrance, beauty, body care, etc.) are usually filled with – you guessed it – women. And, for whatever reason, many guys won't set foot inside these stores – which means even better odds for you!

Single Effort your gift shopping by visiting a women's clothing or personal care store near you. If you're not sure what would be a suitable store to shop in, consider visiting a Bath & Body Works store. Most women like shopping and sampling the fragrances and lotions in a Bath & Body Works, so there should be plenty of women "in store" for you to meet.

In addition to being surrounded by women, something else plays in your favor when you're shopping at a women's store. Women have a natural instinct to help – it's in their DNA. Just like most of us are drawn to fast cars, power tools, and scantily clad beach bodies, many women are nurturers and love to help a man in need.

Similar to finding an ice breaker at a garage sale, when you're in a women's beauty, clothing, or fragrance store and you spot someone you'd like to talk with, walk up to her with a few items in hand and ask her opinion on what you've selected.

Ask questions you know she would enjoy answering – is the blouse you're holding something appropriate for your daughter to wear at a holiday event? Is the perfume you're considering a fragrance that your niece or daughter would enjoy?

Regardless of what you ask, make sure you give her time to answer and let her play out the nurturing role (most likely you'll learn something new as well). Once she's done giving you her opinion move on to another topic and if she's interesting enough, don't leave without her phone number in hand (if you're not sure how to ask for her phone number, the next chapter has your answers!).

Where? Some Parting Thoughts

Keep in mind that it behooves you to put yourself in situations where you can leverage both your physical and non-physical attributes in meeting new women. When you're visiting the same well-worn locations as every other guy, sometimes it's easier to bemoan that you have bad luck meeting new women than to realize that your choice of location could have a lot to do with your odds.

As the 17th-century satirist Jonathan Swift once pronounced, "I must complain the cards are ill-shuffled till I have a good hand." Instead of waiting for the standard shuffle – the kind every other guy is using – to deal you a good hand, stack the deck in your favor. Seek out creative and unique locations to attract and meet new women – doubling down on your captivating charm, wit, and intelligence alongside your striking good looks!

CHAPTER 9

Approaching and Talking to Women (KISS)

For those who remember the movie *Top Gun*, the main character, Maverick (Tom Cruise), is instructed to "Call the ball" while attempting to land his jet on an aircraft carrier. "Call the ball" is a real-world U.S. Navy communication sent by the control tower to an aircraft pilot. It refers to the pilot sighting the "ball," or light, on the deck of a carrier that lets him know he's on the correct flight path for landing his plane.

Just like landing a plane on an aircraft carrier, you (as the pilot) need to "Call the ball" to ensure you're on the right approach when talking to women you meet in chance encounters. And just like flying a jet, it's not the takeoff or the flight itself that's the most formidable, but the landing.

You've visited all the right waypoints during your flight – locations where the women outnumber the men and your odds of meeting Ms. Right are the greatest. Now you'd like to land a conversation with the pretty woman you see standing next to you. You want it to be a conversation that says,

"You're interesting and I'd like to know more about you," but at the same time isn't too pushy or corny. You want to be remembered after the conversation is over – but only for the right reasons.

Like flying a jet, this is where many guys will fail to "Call the ball" and as a result, botch their final approach to landing a conversation on the deck of the USS New Encounter.

There are many things to consider. How do you approach the woman you want to talk to? How do you introduce yourself? Does appearance matter? How do you keep that first conversation flowing and natural but at the same time short and to the point?

Things can get complicated and spiral out of control quickly when you're talking to a woman you just met and don't know what to say. Indeed, there are entire books written on the subject of how to talk to a woman – what to say and, sometimes more importantly, what *not* to say.

If you wanted to boil this chapter down to one word it would be "simple." The secret to striking up a meaningful conversation with someone you've just met is simple, because "simple" is the key to a great conversation. A rock band could probably say it best – Keep It Simple, Stupid (KISS)! ("Stupid" being used in the most gentle, well-intentioned way, of course!)

To dive in a bit deeper, you need only remember four basic elements to create a great conversation and a lasting first impression with every woman you meet:

1. Mind your appearance
2. Approach with confidence
3. Create an interesting dialogue
4. Leave her wanting more

Mind Your Appearance

First and foremost, when you want to talk with a woman you've just met in a chance encounter, realize that appearance matters. Your first impression will be made before you even say a word. As mentioned earlier, we all judge people by their appearances – it's not entirely proper but it's the world we live in.

This hit home for me recently while looking for a place to park at a local Walmart. As I circled the lot, I noticed a woman in the next aisle pulling her vehicle into a handicapped spot. After parking, we found ourselves walking into the store at the same time – and she appeared to be walking without a problem.

"How rude!" I thought and decided to take it upon myself to say something. "Excuse me," I said. "I noticed you parked in a handicapped spot but you seem to be walking just fine. Shouldn't you park somewhere else?"

The woman looked up at me quite sheepishly – obviously flushed with embarrassment. "I have Stage 2 lung cancer and can't breathe well, so I need to park close to the doors," she said. "I have a handicapped sticker in my car if you'd like to see it."

Boy did I feel like a complete bonehead! I'd made a judgment based on nothing but appearance – and caused this lady a great deal of un-needed embarrassment.

This is just one example of something that happens every day. Though the context will likely be different, women will evaluate you based on your appearance as well. Do you think a woman would rather talk to a smiling, smartly dressed gentleman or an unkempt, grumpy looking guy with ruffled clothes and worn-out shoes?

You can answer that by posing the following question to yourself – would you prefer to strike up a conversation with a nicely dressed woman with manicured nails and a cute hairstyle or someone who looks like she just rolled out of bed? The point to keep in mind is that appearance matters. Always.

When you go out to places where you think you could meet someone new (and that could be anywhere – the pharmacy, the bookstore, or a quick jaunt to your local McDonald's), mind your appearance. Do your best to make yourself look presentable before you step out the door. You never know where you might bump into someone you'd like to get to know.

Not sure what constitutes presentable? Here's a litmus test to help you decide – I call it the "Paparazzi Test":

> Imagine yourself a movie star (who hasn't done that already?) and that, when you venture from your home, you'll be photographed by the star-chasing paparazzi. If someone took your picture when you stepped out your door, would you be comfortable enough with your dress and appearance to have your picture posted on the cover of a tabloid? If your look passes the Paparazzi Test, you're good to go!

Of course what constitutes a good look will depend on what you like to wear and where it is you'll be going. If you're meeting a woman for a date, a nice pair of jeans or dress pants and a casual dress shirt would be appropriate for most outings – like a stroll through an art gallery, an evening at an open-air jazz festival, or simply a quiet dinner together at a nice restaurant. However, you'd likely opt for more casual attire, like nice shorts and a short-sleeve shirt, if plans involved something with a bit more physical activity like hiking a nature trail or visiting a pumpkin patch to pick pumpkins together.

Note that being ready for a date or chance encounter isn't just about your appearance. How you smell is important, too. Most women love a good-quality cologne, so consider embracing a nice-smelling pheromone. Just a dab or spritz or two will suffice. Too much of a good thing is a bad thing in this case – use common "scents" and don't overdo it!

Regardless of your destination (on a date night or not), take a few minutes to review your "look" before you step out the door. Check your appearance through the lens of others and you'll always be prepared to make a great impression!

Show Some Sole!

Whether you're on a date or it's a chance first encounter, you want your wardrobe to help you (not hinder you) in making a great impression. Believe it or not, it all starts from the bottom up – with your shoes.

Most women love shoes – they're lovers of the sole – and they will judge their dates (at least in part) by the shoes they keep. So a pair of quality leather shoes is a must. In fact, if you can afford it, consider owning two pair – one brown and one black – to allow for more flexibility in your attire.

For those without fickle feet who can order shoes online without trying them on first, one of the best sources for shoes is Zappos (**www.zappos.com**). They have a large selection of men's shoes and offer free shipping on all your shoe purchases. In addition, if you don't like the shoes after they arrive you can return them within 365 days for a credit or refund (there are a few caveats on returns so make sure you check their website for details).

*If you prefer to try on your shoes before buying them, DSW Shoes (also online at **www.dsw.com**) is a great choice – and don't let their marketing hinder you. Although they position themselves primarily as a women's store, they carry a wide variety of men's shoes as well. And this very much works to your advantage – you get the Single Effort benefit of shopping in a store packed with like-minded, sole-loving women!*

Looking for a few "well-worn" rules to help you determine what color footwear should be worn with your current ensemble? Coordinate your dating (and day-to-day) attire with confidence using this foolproof three-step process:

1. Select a pair of pants
2. Coordinate the color of your shoes, socks, and belt to the color of your pants
3. Tie in your shirt (color and style) with your bottom half (shoes, socks, belt, and pants)

For example, if you've selected a dark grey set of slacks, you should wear black shoes, black or grey dress socks, and a black belt. Conversely, if you're going to wear khaki slacks, wear brown shoes, brown or khaki dress socks, and a brown belt.

A table should help bring it all together:

Pant Color	Shoe Color	Sock Color	Belt Color
Darker colors like black and grey	Black	Black or Grey	Black
Lighter colors like khaki and brown	Brown	Khaki or Brown	Brown
Jeans	Black or Brown	Match Shoes	Match Shoes

A color-matching table for a single guy's wardrobe

When selecting socks and shoes to wear on a date, keep two additional points in mind:

- Leave the white athletic (tube) socks at home. With the exception of an outing that involves physical activity (biking, jogging, tennis, etc.) treat white socks as you would your prized bug collection – keep them far away from your date!
- If your shoes are scuffed or look worn out, make a point of spending five minutes polishing them before you leave the house. And when your date has concluded, remember to use a shoe tree to keep them looking and smelling great for next time.

Hair Today…

Beyond clothing and shoes, proper grooming will go a long way in contributing to an eye-catching first impression. Three main hair-growth areas deserve your immediate attention. The first is an area many guys ignore, but which more and more women are taking notice of, i.e. the hair in and around a man's "lower regions." Women have been shaving and trimming this area for years and societal norms are now allowing men to follow suit. Many women now find a smooth, trimmed look on male bodies more attractive.

Among the women I've dated where this topic has come up (surprisingly, more often than one would think – and a good sign the date was progressing well!), most did indeed prefer the "groomed look" on a guy. Not entirely shaved off, mind you, just a well-kempt look.

I've tried several shavers for body grooming and the product that has worked best for me is the Philips Norelco Professional Body Grooming System (BG2030). The Philips

Norelco shaver is a cordless, rechargeable electric shaver that comes with several attachments to address different hair types and shaving regions on men. I've never experienced a nick or cut using the Philips Norelco – definitely Single Effort tested and approved!

The Philips Norelco Professional Body Grooming System (BG2030)

(Reproduced with the permission of Koninklijke Philips Electronics N.V. and Philips Electronics North America Corporation. All rights reserved.)

One note of caution, however – do NOT use a *facial* hair electric razor in and around your groin. Instead, use a razor like the Philips Norelco that's specifically designed for this area. If you fail to heed this caution, you could wind up singing some serious blues when you accidentally grab some extra skin (that would be the sound of an "Ewww," followed immediately by an "Ouch!" and then a "@#$%!").

In addition to your groin, two other areas are often overlooked by men (sometimes even more so than the lower regions), namely the nose and ears. To be sure, we all have nose and ear hairs and they serve a valuable function. They're there to act as a natural filter for the dust, dirt, and pollen drifting in the air. But just because these hairs occur naturally, doesn't mean they should be left to grow unchecked.

Grass looks nice on a lawn when it's manicured – but not so much when it's three feet tall. The same is true for your nose and ear hairs. They have a purpose but should be trimmed regularly. Most women consider it a turn off for a guy to have hair poking out of his nose or sprouting from his ears.

Years ago, it was pointed out to me that hair was starting to creep out from my nostrils and ears – just enough to be noticeable when viewed up close. Being new to the concept of nose and ear hair trimming, I really believed such things were a waste of time.

Now, several years later as a single guy, I'm a hair trimming convert. Trimming your nose and ears not only gives a cleaner look (that virtually all ladies will appreciate) but as a side benefit, trimmed nose hair also allows for a bit easier breathing through the nostrils.

There are many nose and ear hair groomers on the market and they all do about the same (good) job. A quick Amazon search on the keywords "nose hair trimmer" or "ear hair trimmer" will yield many results. If you're looking for more concrete advice, consider purchasing a quality set of tweezers for your ears and a battery-powered trimmer for your nose (many times, battery-powered nose trimmers are easier and faster to use than manual trimmers).

Remember, your first impression will be made without you ever saying a word. Instead of lamenting the fact that you don't like to be judged by your looks, choose to embrace the fact and use it to your advantage. Mae West, the American actress and screenwriter (and an all-around sex symbol for her time) once said, "It's better to be looked over than overlooked." Indeed – if you're going to be judged, you might as well be judged good looking!

Approach with Confidence

Not only is appearance important when you speak to a woman for the first time, but your attitude is also key. This is where the second element to creating a great conversation and lasting first impression comes in – approaching with confidence. Not too much as there's a fine line between confidence and arrogance, but enough to say, "I know you'll like me if you just take the time to get to know me."

The crucial difference between confidence and arrogance is intent. If your intent is to try to impress someone with how self-confident, smart, or important you are, you'll come across as arrogant. Focus instead on learning about the other person. When a woman first meets you, she doesn't want to know about your many accomplishments. Her objective is much more straightforward – she simply wants to find you interesting and for you to be interested in her.

To come in at the right level of confidence in a conversation with a woman you just met, remind yourself, just before talking to her, that you're a great catch – but also resist the temptation to review everything you've ever done and seen. Remember that confident people are completely comfortable with others knowing nothing about their accomplishments.

In addition, as mentioned in chapter 2, finding the true "you" before you begin dating (and avoiding the rebound effect) is extremely important. If you know what you want in a partner, you'll come across as much more confident in your conversations with women. Remember that a confident guy doesn't *need* a woman, he *wants* a woman. And women often have a keen sense of this.

If you don't have the confidence yet to approach a woman you want to talk to, start building it. How? Just like studying to play a musical instrument or learning how to swim, you need to move out of your comfort zone and practice. You don't become a good swimmer by dipping your toe into the pool every so often – you need to jump in and take some strokes. And so it goes with building your confidence in talking to women.

Move outside your comfort zone and make a point of talking to different women every day to build your confidence, no matter where you find yourself – in line at a store checkout, waiting for your table at a restaurant, or filling up at a gas station. Use every opportunity you have to practice talking to women and building your confidence.

It doesn't need to be a long dialogue, either. It could be as simple as saying "Hello" to someone you find attractive and interesting (KISS). When you appear confident you give off signals that you're also appealing and engaging, and everyone wants to be around an appealing, engaging guy – especially women!

Create an Interesting Dialogue

You have the look and you've built up the confidence to have a conversation with someone new. Now you need to take it to the next level and capture her interest by utilizing the third element and actually landing an interesting conversation.

Many guys fail to "Call the ball" at this stage because they try to figure out the ideal conversation beforehand. Do your best to avoid this. It rarely if ever works. Instead, deliver one simple and genuine compliment to get the conversation rolling (KISS).

A compliment can be a very powerful tool in meeting new women – but it needs to be sincere. And you need to deliver it confidently, with good eye contact, and with no apologies. If you give a compliment with these suggestions in mind there's a good chance the woman you've met will be eager to learn more about you.

A keen thing to remember when delivering a compliment (and just plain common sense) is to stay away from complimenting a woman's shape or other physical assets, like her breasts or butt. This will just make her feel like an object (women can tell when a compliment is a come-on) and the conversation will most likely be over before it ever had a chance to begin.

Here are some examples of straightforward compliments that you can use to open up a dialogue with a woman (regardless of where you might meet her):

- I couldn't help but notice when we met – you have great eyes.
- Excuse me – I just wanted to tell you that you have a beautiful smile.
- I love the color of your dress – it really highlights your pretty eyes.
- I just had to walk over and tell you that I think you're very graceful – you carry yourself beautifully.
- I really admire a woman with class and style – and just had to say "Hi!"

Once you deliver your sincere compliment, she'll most likely thank you. If she's interested in continuing a dialogue, follow three simple tips that will help you land a great conversation:

1. Focus on your "now" moment
2. Try to integrate one of your interests or passions into the conversation
3. End with a question

These three tips will flow quickly and effortlessly with just a little practice.

On one occasion, while shopping at my local grocery store, I noticed a cute woman in the sauce and spices section. She was standing in the middle of the aisle holding two different salsa bottles in her hands, trying to figure out which brand to purchase. I approached her and said, "Excuse me. I noticed you from across the aisle. You carry yourself beautifully – and I just had to say 'Hi.'"

She thanked me for the compliment and turned to face me (indicating her willingness to talk with me further – tell-tale body cues are covered in chapter 11). I continued by saying, "I see you're looking at salsas. I much prefer the brand in your left hand when making homemade tacos."

This was my "now" conversation – it was something she was interested in at that moment. It had immediate relevance, so she listened to what I was saying. However, it wasn't the salsa I was after – it was getting to know her – so I was ready to move into the next part of the conversation by integrating a passion or interest into the discussion.

Why integrate a passion or interest? Passion breeds energy and excitement. When you talk about something you're genuinely interested in, your energy level will rise. And when your energy level rises, hers will too. Passion breeds excitement and excitement is contagious – infecting her with the desire to get to know you!

Regardless of your energy level, there is one piece of advice that is even *more* important when talking to women (in a chance encounter, on a date, or at any other time) and should always be kept top of mind: *look into a woman's eyes when talking to her.* A guy whose eyes wander past the woman he's talking to (presumably checking out the other women in the room)

– or a guy who speaks to a woman's chest instead of her face – is not going to meet with much success. It's a sure-fire way to miss the ball and botch your landing.

Back to the woman holding the salsa bottles. I'd had my "now" conversation with her and wanted to move on to something I was energized about. Because I'd already mentioned homemade tacos, I decided to integrate my passion for cooking into the dialogue. I continued the conversation by saying, "I recently made tacos at home with the salsa you have in your left hand and my kids really enjoyed them! I think they preferred the milder flavor."

Now it was time to see if I could keep the conversation flowing by asking a question. By asking a question you lower any barriers to a continued conversation. You make it easy for her to know how to respond back to you.

"Are you planning on tacos as well?" I asked. At this point I could feel my energy level rising – and I could sense hers was, too!

Leave Her Wanting More

You've moved through the stages of creating a good look for yourself and shoring up your confidence, and you've just started a dialogue with someone who interests you. All systems are go, but you'll need to maintain your approach in order to touch down on the carrier USS New Encounter with her phone number and the promise of a date in hand. The key to a good landing – and the fourth component in creating a winning dialogue and a great first impression – is not to overstay your welcome.

There's a great episode in season nine of *Seinfeld* titled "The Burning" where George Costanza (Jason Alexander) decides he's tired of having his conversations end on a sour note. In this episode, George always says something very witty early on in a conversation and then screws things up later by saying something equally awkward or embarrassing.

To remedy the problem, George devises a plan to end every conversation on a "high note" and leave the people he's talking to wanting more. So anytime he says something witty or funny he then leaves – immediately – abruptly ending the conversation so as not to risk putting his foot in his mouth. His plan works, much to the chagrin of the people he's talking to, who now can't wait to hear more of what George has to say.

To a degree, your behavior in a conversation with a woman you've just met needs to model George's. You want to have an engaging and witty conversation but not overstay your welcome. If you stay too long, you could come across as desperate or needy – definitely not the type of impression you want to make.

A good rule of thumb – I call it "George's Ten-Minute Rule" – is to spend no more than ten minutes talking to someone you've just met in a chance encounter. This forces you to be straightforward and succinct. Near the end of the conversation (or the ten-minute mark, whichever comes first), if you feel a connection, ask for her phone number and thank her for the conversation – then politely excuse yourself.

How do you go about requesting a woman's phone number? It's simple – just ask. Ask her for her phone number with one or two sentences, with confidence and without apology. Don't ramble on trying to find a cute or witty way to ask for her number. Be succinct and to the point (KISS).

After I was done talking about homemade tacos with the woman holding the salsa bottles I decided I'd like to get to know her better. I said to her, "I enjoyed our conversation and would like to get to know you more – could I have your phone number?" and she gave it to me without hesitation.

Note that I didn't say I'd call her that night or the next day. I wanted to leave her intrigued by our conversation and a bit off balance not knowing exactly *when* I would call.

In a chance conversation with a woman you just met you want to go out like George Costanza – always leave her wanting more!

So Long! So What? Move On.

You've followed all the rules – you're looking sharp, you've approached with confidence, and you've enjoyed an engaging conversation – but she balked at giving you her phone number. She's simply not interested. Sometimes the chemistry isn't there and there's nothing you can do about it. It's time to say, "So long! So what? Move on." (And do so without a second thought.)

No matter how hard you try, there are just some women who will not be interested in you. Chin up, however, because there are hundreds if not thousands more for you to meet.

When faced with rejection by a woman many guys count it as a loss, and you may be tempted to do the same. Instead, consider making lemonade from the lemons you've been dealt. Learn from each encounter that didn't go the way you wanted. Think back on what you could've done better and work to improve your odds for your next encounter.

One thing to avoid is the impulse to keep pestering a woman when she's made her lack of interest clear. A sure-fire way to turn a woman off (faster than opening a conversation with "So...how much *do* you weigh?") is looking or acting desperate. If you're not getting any traction in your conversation or she's flat out told you she's not interested then stop pursuing her.

Ron White, a gifted comedian who's lived through his share of marriages and divorces, does a great job boiling it down: "I believe if life gives you lemons, make lemonade – then find someone that life gave vodka to and have a party!" If you don't have a connection with someone, move on – find someone who's got your vodka and make your own party!

One more thing: there's absolutely no guarantee that every encounter you have with a woman will end in success. Indeed, many chance encounters will *not* end with the promise of a continuing dialogue (to which I can personally attest). She may say "Yes" to giving you her phone number, she may say "No," but there *is* one guarantee you can count on. If you don't ask, the answer will *always* be "No."

To sum up, in a chance conversation with a woman you've just met remember the mantra – simple is always better (KISS) Whether you've run into her at a party or you're talking to her in the checkout line at the pet store, the guidelines are always the same:

1. Appearance matters – nice clothing and good grooming make all the difference
2. Confidence is key – practice, practice, practice
3. Capture her interest – open with a compliment, focus on your "now" moment, and bring in a passion
4. Don't hang around too long – leave her wanting more!

Keep these guidelines in mind for great conversations and first impressions. Be your own Maverick when it comes to meeting new women. Kick the tires and light the fires. Enjoy the flight and have a smooth landing!

CHAPTER 10

Before You Begin Dating...

After meeting an interesting woman, either in person or online (tips and recommendations for how to thrive in the online dating scene follow in chapter 12), you'll most likely want to move to the next step and set up your first date. In at least one sense, first dates are very similar to chance encounters. You want to make a great first impression and, if the chemistry is right, leave her craving more – thus opening up the possibility of future dates.

In another sense, a first date couldn't be more contrary to a chance encounter. With a chance encounter, expectations are generally minimal. With a planned date, on the other hand, you've probably both thought through your upcoming time together (perhaps at length) and you each have an expectation of how it should turn out. The heat, as they say, is on.

Just like with cooking, there's a bit of preparation that must take place to make sure you don't get burned – to ensure that all your dates (first, second, and beyond) turn out to be as enjoyable and successful as possible. A bit of dating *mise en place*, as it were.

First dates (and dating in general) can sometimes be tricky to navigate, so take some time to think through the eventualities before you begin. When it comes to first dates, you want to make sure all the components that make for a great experience are ready well before your time together. That you've prepared yourself for both happy and unhappy surprises, that you're ready to lead with a Good Knight mindset, and for those with kids – that you've established some ground rules early on to keep their best interests at heart.

And once you've set the stage with the proper preparation? You'll be ready to cook up a date she won't soon forget!

A Good Knight Revisited

Before you begin dating it's important to establish a proper Good Knight mindset. As mentioned early on in the book, this means incorporating chivalry into your daily life so that being chivalrous on dates just comes naturally. What is chivalry in today's world? It means doing what your mother taught you – treating women with respect and courtesy.

Here are a few examples of chivalrous behavior:
- Opening doors for a woman wherever you may be – in a parking lot, at a restaurant, or at the mall
- Pulling out and pushing in her chair at dinner
- Picking up the tab on a first or second date (a lively topic discussed a bit later in this chapter)
- Holding an umbrella over her head when you're walking in the rain
- Giving her your coat when it's cold outside
- Letting her be the first to walk into a room
- Ensuring she gets home safely after a date

Learning to be a Good Knight is simple. There are just two key tenets of knighthood:
1. Never expect anything in return for your chivalry
2. Apply chivalry in *all* your interactions with women

The first tenet is to never expect anything in return for your Good Knight behavior. Just like a compliment, your chivalry needs to be sincere. Otherwise, women will recognize that you're just being nice in hopes of getting something in return. If your Good Knight attitude is genuine and from the heart, however, your words and actions will show it – and women will be impressed!

Even though you should never expect anything in return for your Good Knight behavior, you'll receive an entire range of responses from women. Some won't acknowledge your chivalry while others will respond with a kind "Thank You." If you're lucky enough to receive a "Thank You," accept it genuinely and modestly – here too women will be able to tell if you're not sincere or are patting yourself on the back too much for a simple courtesy.

If you don't receive a response, don't let it sway you from being a Good Knight. Lack of response could be due to a number of factors outside your control: shyness, a degree of misplaced embarrassment, or even surprise (some women will have never experienced genuine chivalry before, which is great for you – they'll remember you as their "first"!).

Regardless of any lack of response you may encounter, most women *adore* a Good Knight. If you need proof, ask any woman you know if she'd appreciate someone opening a car door for her (better yet, ask her the last time it was done for her). Even when a woman fails to acknowledge your chivalry, take heart – she'll definitely remember you for it!

The second tenet to being a Good Knight is to apply chivalry in *all* your interactions with women. Not just with women you want to date or are dating – but every woman you interact with on a daily basis. Whether you're on a date or having a casual conversation with someone in line next to you at the bank, practice chivalry every day so it becomes second nature.

For example, are you leaving a store with a woman close behind you? Hold the door open for her. Are you entering a conference room at work next to a woman? Let her be the first to walk in.

Keep in mind, however, that being a Good Knight takes work. It's a journey more than an end state. As you practice the Good Knight way of life, chivalry will start to become second nature – but it'll always require some effort on your part.

I've made many mistakes along the road to Knighthood. On one occasion, my date stood patiently at the entrance to a restaurant while I stood behind her, oblivious to the fact that she was waiting for me to open the door for her. On another, I made my date walk through the rain after a day of shopping – only to witness rain-soaked mascara running down her face when we finally got into my car.

There have been many other instances, however, where being a Good Knight just came naturally. One afternoon I was pushing my near-empty shopping cart through my local Target (by the way, Target stores are often "target rich" with women) when I spotted a woman I'd never met. She was walking toward me at a hurried pace, heading for the checkout lanes with an arm-load of items.

As we neared each other I saw she wasn't going to make it to the checkout without losing at least a couple items to gravity. I quickly pushed my shopping cart up to her and invited her to put everything she was carrying into my cart. I told her it looked like she needed the cart more than I did and that I'd get another one. She was very grateful and thanked me before continuing on her way.

Adopting a Good Knight mindset will make performing chivalrous acts second nature. With a little practice, your chivalry will shine through on all your dates and in all your interactions with women – helping you stand out from the sea of other men your date has already encountered. And who knows? After a great date, being a Good Knight might even lead to a "good night" for both of you!

Your Dating Kit

Dating is fun and exciting, but you won't always know what to expect. As you get ready to date women it's important that you arrive prepared. A dating kit is a small (and discreet) set of items placed in a bag or pouch (nothing fancy – a simple Ziploc sandwich bag will do) and stored in your vehicle's console or glove box. Its purpose is threefold: 1) to prepare you for the unexpected, 2) to help you avoid potentially embarrassing situations, and 3) to give you a leg up on ensuring your date is successful.

A dating kit consists of four essential items that should accompany you on every date:

1. Breath fresheners
2. Colgate® Wisp® (a small, single-use mini-brush)
3. Condoms
4. A compliment

The first item to go into your dating kit should be breath fresheners like mint-flavored gum, Certs, Tic Tacs, or breath strips. It's an uncomfortable feeling when you're moving in for that first kiss and suddenly realize your date could be overwhelmed, not by your passion or charm, but by the garlic odor radiating from your mouth after the spaghetti dinner you just finished.

Better to ensure your mouth is fresh before the kiss. As the saying goes, you only get one chance to make a great first impression!

The second item in your dating kit should be a couple of Colgate Wisp mini-brushes, an invaluable last-minute dating aid. A Wisp is a single-use mini-brush that doesn't require water or rinsing. There's no need for water because the mini-brush contains a small freshening bead which dissolves in use.

Let's say you're at work and have arranged a last-minute date but don't have time to return home to freshen up. Before you leave for your date, take 30 seconds and use a Wisp mini-brush to dislodge any leftover food particles that may have wedged themselves in your teeth.

A Wisp mini-brush can also be used once your date has commenced. After you've completed your meal on a breakfast, lunch, or dinner date, consider excusing yourself to the men's room to freshen your smile with a quick cleaning. A Wisp mini-brush is the size of a small pocket knife – easily stored in your dating kit bag or on your person (e.g. in a pants pocket).

The Colgate Wisp – a great dating kit accessory!

(© Colgate-Palmolive at www.colgatepalmolive.com)

The third item in your dating kit is something that we, as guys, know well but sometimes forget or are reluctant to carry – a condom. It may be wishful thinking but you never know when your date could progress into something more intimate. Remind yourself to grab a pack of condoms while you're at the store picking up your Wisps and breath fresheners. Keep a pack handy in your dating kit, and at least one condom on your person, anytime you venture out on a date. (note: condoms can degrade over time – play it safe and replace your condoms every six months or so to ensure you're protected when they're needed).

A good place to carry a condom on your person is in your pants pocket or a business card holder. Be careful about placing a condom in your wallet, however. If you take your wallet out during the date and the condom is visible or falls out, well, it could be awkward for both of you (alternatively, with the right woman, it could also be a great conversation starter!).

The fourth and final item to include in your dating kit is not something you buy or carry but something you give – a compliment. Make a point of passing along at least one sincere compliment to your date during your time together. Just like in a chance encounter when you're trying to strike up a conversation, your compliment should be genuine and to the point (KISS).

On a date you'll have more time to put together your compliment than you do in a chance encounter – so take a moment to notice something special. For instance, if it's obvious your date is sporting freshly manicured nails, let her know how nice they look. Noticing and then complimenting a woman on something she's put effort into for your date will make her feel appreciated and cast you in a positive light.

Bear in mind, however, that facts are not compliments. Statements like "I see you're wearing a new dress," "Those shoes sure are bright," or "Your hair is much shorter in real life than in your picture" do not, unfortunately, count as compliments. For it to be considered a compliment, you need to say something nice about your date. Be sure to use pleasing and engaging (but sincere) adjectives in your compliment (and no, "bright" doesn't qualify – unless you're talking about her radiant smile!).

Keep in mind that women hear compliments about their looks all the time. Instead of focusing on outward beauty, you may want to consider going to the next level and focusing on something else that makes your date beautiful in your eyes – it could be her smile, the way she walks, or even her attitude. For example, "It's really rare to meet someone who's willing to launch a new career and follow their dream. So many people are afraid to take risks – I really admire that about you."

And finally, just like in a chance encounter, try to end your compliment with a short question. A question will help keep the conversation flowing and will give your date an opportunity to talk about something she enjoys. For example, "I love that necklace – it really highlights your pretty blue eyes. Where did you get it?"

As previously noted, sincerity and genuine intent will always take you further than comments and questions designed solely to score points. Try to compliment your date on something you really admire and can show a genuine interest in talking about.

On the other side of the coin, one item that should not be included in your dating kit is your constantly ringing and text message beeping cell phone. It's fine to bring your mobile phone on a date but don't place it in plain sight next to you or have it constantly ringing with phone calls or beeping with text messages. Be a Good Knight and focus on your "now" moment. A noisy cell phone interrupts the flow of your conversation and tells your date she doesn't have your full focus and attention.

Instead, set your phone on vibrate and place it in your pocket – out of sight but still accessible if you receive an emergency call or text message. If you need to have your phone visible or have to check it from time to time – for example, maybe you're expecting a good night call from your kids or an important call from work that can't be missed – let your date know at the beginning of your time together so she understands that you're not ignoring or disrespecting her.

Who Pays for What?

When you consider what to expect from dating, it's a good idea to spend a little time thinking about how it will impact your finances. This will likely involve a look at your money and how and when you want to spend it. More specifically, you (or your date) will eventually ask, "Who pays for what?"

There are sound arguments on both sides of this question. On the one hand, in this age of equal rights a woman should be expected to shoulder her fair share of the dating costs. On the other, chivalry is still appreciated and the guy, as a matter of etiquette, may still be expected to foot the bill.

My own recommendation is to land somewhere between the two extremes. This means that, as a guy, you should pay for the first, second, and possibly the third date – but then the cost of dates should be shared.

There are several reasons for this approach. One is that, while picking up the tab for a date may be a relic of a time gone by, it still has redeeming value. It demonstrates that you're a gentleman and is an expression of etiquette and courtesy – it shows a Good Knight mindset.

For those who've gone through a divorce and have ended up with an unwanted obligation to pay large helpings of spousal support – take a deep breath on this next one. Hold back the desire to scream until you've read all the way through. Ready? Now inhale!

Another important reason for picking up the tab on the first couple dates is that it lets a woman know you can provide for her. This is a crucial concern for many women, who are trying to gauge whether you're "long-term-relationship material."

Keep in mind, however, that this is not to suggest that you *should* or *would* provide for her (quite the opposite, as many guys feel that a woman should be able to support herself). But the *feeling* of knowing that a man *can* provide – the realization that she's with a provider – is a very important emotional need that many women have.

OK. *Now* you can exhale. That wasn't so bad, was it? Those of us who've been obliged to pay spousal or child support from a divorce situation can be especially prickly when the conversation appears to turn into a rationalization of why a man should support a woman – definitely not the case here though, so you can rest easy!

Even if you're *not* looking for a long-term relationship it can still be beneficial to be viewed as a potential provider in her eyes. You'll likely be placed in the "more favorable" category and you'll find that it can afford you certain privileges and perks beyond being seen as a possible long-term mate. For example, your date will be more open to splitting the tab when you go out (after the first couple dates), more willing to accompany you to events organized at the last minute, and less likely to cancel dates in the eleventh hour – all good things!

Of course, there will be some women who will insist on paying their own way – even on a Mini-Date (a Mini-Date is a low-stress, low-cost first date with someone new discussed in detail in the next chapter). If your date insists on paying her portion then definitely let her. Many times a woman will pay her own way simply to maintain a level of comfort – so as not to feel a sense of obligation later.

There's also another option if you find a date is progressing well and you really want to see her again. If she offers to pick up the bill respond with, "How about you pick up the tab next time?" She'll appreciate your chivalry and you'll immediately get a sense of whether she wants to see you again as well!

If you're dating someone who constantly allows you to pick up the tab, however, at some point the free ride should end (unless you have strong feelings the other way). In this age of equal rights a man shouldn't have to foot the bill forever. After the second or third outing consider having a conversation around equalizing the costs of future get-togethers.

There are several benefits to splitting the costs:
- It helps lessen the obligation a woman might otherwise feel afterward
- It spreads the financial burden across the both of you
- It signals that she's ready to "invest" in the relationship

Sometimes splitting a bill on a date can be awkward though, so consider taking turns paying. Maybe she picks up the tab for dinner and you pick up the cost of tickets and drinks for the comedy show after.

If she doesn't agree to split the tab after several dates, that could say something about her mindset – and might give you pause as you consider whether or not you want to sign up for the long haul.

With the right woman – if you're respectful and up front about expectations – splitting the cost of future dates might make you stand out as someone who is refreshingly honest and even *increase* her desire to be with you. It allows your date to maintain a certain independence and see herself as an equal partner in the relationship. At the end of the day, she may end up respecting you even more!

Some Additional Tips

As you enter the dating scene, on your first date and beyond, a few basic Do's and Don'ts will help you create a fun and engaging atmosphere while you and your date are getting to know one another.

Here are some established dating tips that should serve you well:

DO try to keep things upbeat and fun. Choose conversation topics that help you learn more about your date – her hobbies, friends, where she grew up, or where she's recently traveled. Stay away from heavy or sensitive subjects like religion, marriage, politics, or money.

DON'T focus in on past relationships. It's fine to briefly discuss your prior situation (e.g. a recent breakup or divorce) but then quickly move on to other topics.

DO look into her eyes when either of you are talking. As mentioned earlier, keep your eyes fixed on her and not on your surroundings or the scenery walking by.

DON'T do all the talking. Take a breather – let her drive at least half the conversation.

DON'T be shy. Ask questions, and pay attention to her answers. You're on the date to learn more about her, so be naturally inquisitive.

DO dress nicely (visit chapter 9 for dress and grooming refreshers). If nothing else, remember the Paparazzi Test!

DON'T complain in excess. If the food you're eating stinks or the location you're at is not what it was supposed to be, no harm in mentioning it but then move on to another topic. No one likes a whiner.

DO remember to pack your dating kit – and the all-important compliment!

DON'T shut down if you're not instantly attracted to her when you meet for the first time. Sometimes it takes a little while to warm up to someone new. Consider staying through the date to see if your initial assessment changes. You don't want to cut yourself out too quickly from someone who could end up being a great catch!

DO stay confident. Don't worry if you feel a little shy – your date will most likely be just as nervous as you.

DON'T forget your manners. This is where being a Good Knight will pay off!

DON'T try to reveal everything about yourself on a first date. Keep an air of mystery about you – be like George Costanza and leave her wanting more!

Establishing Ground Rules When Kids Are Involved

This last consideration is for the dads in the audience. For those with children, it's a good idea to establish some ground rules for yourself before you begin dating, rules that have your children's best interests at heart.

There are many scenarios to take into account when you're a dad who's also interested in dating. Ultimately, the question "Is this in the best interest of my children?" can serve as your litmus test, but here are some additional pointers:

DO take time out for yourself to meet and date women when you feel you're ready. You don't have to live the life of a hermit until your children reach adulthood. Go out and have some fun!

DON'T date and have fun at your children's expense, however. Limit your dating to the days when you don't have parenting time with your kids. Keep the time you have with your kids exclusive to them. And if your date doesn't understand and instead just pouts and whines that she isn't getting enough attention? Well, it might be time to say, "So long! So what? Move on."

DON'T introduce your kids to every person you date. Most experts agree that doing so will only confuse them and foster resentment. However...

DO consider introducing your kids to your date after you've been in an exclusive and committed relationship for several months. Do so with a short activity (1-2 hours) held in a neutral setting. Your kids might feel uncomfortable spending the entire day with someone they just met or having a strange person show up in their home to meet them.

DON'T have sleepovers with a date when the children are present. Also, having a date stop by after your children are asleep is a very risky move – if your kids wake up and find an unfamiliar person in the house, the aftermath can be quite unpleasant for all parties involved. See the second rule above and keep your time with your kids exclusive to them.

CHAPTER 11

Your Two First Dates

With dating kit in tow, your Good Knight mindset in place, and some important Do's and Don'ts under your belt, your first date with someone new will eventually arrive. When the time comes, try to avoid the word "big" – steer clear of anything that will involve a big time commitment or a big outlay of cash.

Instead, consider doing something that doesn't consume an entire evening and is inexpensive. For example, instead of dinner at a fancy restaurant, make plans to grab a coffee or a light snack together at a local sandwich shop.

Why? If the chemistry between you isn't there or she simply isn't your type, you can extricate yourself quickly – without spending a lot of money or wasting any more of your time (or hers for that matter). In addition, when you choose an inexpensive setting for your first date, it's easier to gauge whether your date is genuinely interested in you or simply enamored with the location.

My big lesson learned on picking the right location for a first date is the $75 I spent on a dinner date with a woman who turned out to be at least 75 pounds over her ideal weight ($1 per pound, I know, plenty of irony).

The problem I had was not her weight per se, but that she'd misrepresented herself to me in her pictures prior to meeting in person. She had passed herself off as someone much more toned and in shape than she actually was (she'd only sent me upper torso pictures that, as it turned out, were very outdated).

Because she wasn't completely honest with me leading up to our time together, I didn't want to pursue a second date with her. I didn't want to hurt her feelings during the date, however, so I stayed through dinner – even though I had quite a few thoughts of bailing out early.

Don't get caught up in an expensive first date that isn't going anywhere. First dates are all about chemistry – and if it isn't there, you don't want to be either. Instead, plan for *two* first dates – the first, a low-cost, low-pressure "Mini-Date," and the second, a "First Big Date," to be embarked on only if the Mini-Date is a success and you're both interested in getting to know each other better.

First Date #1 – The Mini-Date and Recommended Locations

The Mini-Date is your first date and should be held at a location that's both inexpensive and easy to leave if you find a woman isn't your type or the chemistry just isn't there. When planning your Mini-Date, stick to activities that cost under $10. I call this the "Chicken Fingers Standard."

While the actual "going out for chicken fingers" date is *not* recommended, your Mini-Date should be almost as inexpensive and equally easy to abandon, if necessary. If you have trouble keeping the dollar amount straight, just remember, if chicken had fingers, they'd undoubtedly have 10, so keep it under 10! If you live in a more expensive location, you may need to adjust upward, however.

Some distinctive suggestions for a great Mini-Date under $10:

- Stop at a cider mill for a donut and a cup of cider
- Sit outdoors on a park bench and talk over a light lunch
- Visit a bookstore for a cup of tea and a chat together
- Grab a quick snack at a local sandwich shop
- Stop at a donut shop for an early morning bagel
- Grab a drink in the evening at your local pub
- Order a latte or cappuccino together at a coffee shop

Keep in mind that the "Mini" in Mini-Date doesn't mean you should have a shortened or hurried conversation. If the chemistry is right, you can sit and talk for hours – and maybe move into lunch or dinner at a new location if you feel a connection.

However, if you want some assurance that your Mini-Date won't drag on longer than it should, consider meeting over lunch during the work day so you'll have a reason to keep the date short if you need to. If the Mini-Date goes well, she'll gladly accept your invitation for a follow-up date – your First Big Date (discussed a bit later in this chapter).

First Date #1 – Time for a First Kiss? (Her Body Language Holds the Key)

When you're on your Mini-Date, if the chemistry is right, there's a good chance that a first kiss might be in order (hello dating kit!). If this seems to be the case, let it happen naturally. Don't try to force it with silly come-ons or dares – and above all, never ask for the first kiss!

Most women still like it when their date takes the initiative. Asking a woman for permission to kiss her will just cast you in an unflattering light – as someone who lacks confidence and is unsure of himself. A first kiss is important so you want to make sure it's done right.

As is the case when shopping for your first post-Cold-War Soviet MiG fighter jet (might as well dream big, right?), if you have to ask then you probably can't afford it. To put it another way, if you have to ask for a first kiss then either the mood isn't right or the chemistry has not yet developed. If the mood isn't right, don't try to force it – wait until later in the date or possibly the next date (or even the next!).

How do you know whether your date likes you and it's a good idea to release that first kiss? Her body language holds the key.

Here are some signs that your date is into you:
- Her body faces you and leans into you when you're talking
- Her focus is only on you – looking into your eyes and smiling often
- She bites her lower lip or places the tip of a fingernail between her lips

- She twirls her hair around her finger when she's talking to you
- She touches you – brushing your arm or touching your shoulder or hand
- She holds your hand when you're walking or sitting down
- She lets her hair down during the date

Don't let a missed signal bar the door of romance on your first date. Watch her body language when considering reaching out for your first kiss – and take the initiative if the moment is right!

First Date #1 – A Thank You Is in Order

Regardless of how your Mini-Date turns out – whether it went exceedingly well or the date fell apart within the first 20 minutes – stay true to your Good Knight mindset once the date is over. Send a "Thank You" text message or email within 24 hours of the date's conclusion.

Your "Thank You" message shouldn't be long and drawn out. Instead, go with something simple and to the point that accurately conveys your feelings.

Why not call instead of sending a text message or an email? Sometimes a phone call can be awkward in the case of missed signals. Maybe you thought the date went really well but she didn't feel any chemistry (or vice versa). Or possibly you don't want to see her again and would prefer not getting drawn into a long conversation as to why.

Unless you know for certain she feels the same as you after the date is over, minimize the possibility of an uncomfortable conversation and stick with a text message or email.

After the conclusion of a Mini-Date with a woman I met online, I knew she wasn't for me. I guess I should've realized that someone with a screen name of "SportyHotChick" would probably not be timid, either. Sure enough, when I emailed her the next day to thank her for the date and to let her know I wasn't interested in a second date, her response was fuming – she was incredulous that I wouldn't see her again. I can only imagine how quickly the conversation would've spiraled out of control if I'd called her instead.

If you feel your Mini-Date has gone well and you'd like to go out with your date again, here are examples of messages you could send her way:

- Thank you for meeting me for breakfast this morning. I had a fantastic time talking with you and I'm looking forward to getting to know you more. Would you be interested in a dinner date next week?
- Thank you for a great time! If you're interested, I would love to see you again.
- I wanted to drop you a quick note to let you know I had a GREAT time getting to know you yesterday. I'd like to go out with you again this weekend if you're interested.
- I wanted to let you know I had a wonderful time talking to you this afternoon. I'm still smiling from our time together. Would you be interested in going out again on Friday?

If your date is interested, she'll definitely respond positively and you can set up your First Big Date. If she doesn't respond there could be many reasons, and there's no need to beat yourself up trying to figure it out. Remember not to pester her for a response. Instead – So long! So what? Move on.

By the same token, if the date *didn't* go well or the chemistry simply wasn't there, a kind "Thank you, but I didn't feel a connection" email or text message is appropriate.

In your message to your date, remain upbeat and positive. Refrain from bringing up anything you didn't like about her or your time spent together. No one likes to hear that someone would prefer not to see them again, so be sensitive to this fact. Remember the Golden Rule – send her the type of message you wouldn't mind getting if the shoe were on the other foot.

Here are a couple examples.

- Thanks for meeting me last night – I enjoyed our time together. Unfortunately, the chemistry I'm looking for wasn't quite there. You're a great catch and I'm sure you'll find the right person soon! Best of luck!
- I enjoyed meeting you yesterday but I don't think we're looking for the same thing. Thanks for spending time with me and I hope you find that special someone you're looking for soon!
- Thanks for the coffee this morning. I had a nice time but I'm looking for something more serious. You seem like a great catch and I wish you the best of luck in finding Mr. Right!

Regardless of whether the date went well or not, a simple, to-the-point "Thank You" email or text message is always appropriate. Remember to send your message within 24 hours of the date concluding to ensure your date clearly understands your feelings and intentions.

First Date #1 – Keep Stepping Up to the Plate

Of course, there's one more possibility – your date might send you an email or text message before you send out yours. If she's interested in another date (and you are as well), you're good to go! Follow up with her and plan your First Big Date.

However, what if you'd like to see her again but she sends you a message indicating she's not interested? No worries. Just remember – So long! So what? Move on. The stark reality is that not every Mini-Date is going to result in a second date. In fact, quite the opposite will most likely be true. You're going to end up with many more "misses" than hits on your Mini-Dates.

Baseball legend Ted Williams once said, "Baseball is the only field of endeavor where a man can succeed three times out of ten and be considered a good performer." According to the Baseball Almanac (**www.baseball-almanac.com**), the career leader for batting average is Hall of Famer Ty Cobb at .366 (36%). This means that for every 10 times at bat Ty only connected with the ball and landed a base hit around three times – and he was one of the best!

Just like in baseball, you'll be doing very well if you have three follow-up dates after 10 Mini-Dates. Finding a connection with a new woman three times out of 10 is a great accomplishment. However, don't get discouraged if your dating average is only one or two follow-up dates after 10 Mini-Dates – that's doing very well, too!

Regardless of your dating average, be your own Ty Cobb and keep stepping up to the plate for another try. You'll eventually connect and knock it out of the park!

First Date #2 – Your First Big Date and Recommended Locations

After a successful Mini-Date, where you've both concluded there's enough chemistry and interest for another get-together, it's time to move on to the First Big Date. This will be your second encounter with your date so you want to make sure you do something unique – something that helps you stand out prominently from the other dates she's already had and reinforces that you think she's special.

Creating a great First Big Date experience is essential to making a good impression. A poorly planned outing might leave your date thinking you're careless, unorganized, or not interested. The effort you put into making your second date a great experience could be the difference between having many more dates together and not seeing her again after the date concludes.

When planning your First Big Date don't leave the options wide open – think of two or three possible activities and then ask your date for her opinion. Most women love a guy who can take the initiative and plan a fun time out together, so show her you can take the lead while also taking her preferences to heart.

One other thing to keep in mind – many women will not be comfortable visiting your home until they've had a chance to get to know you. For this reason, use caution in selecting your home as the location for your second outing. If you're unsure how comfortable your date will be, steer clear and choose another locale until the relationship has progressed.

Here are several First Big Date ideas that are distinctive, inexpensive, and memorable:

Enjoy a leisurely stroll through an art gallery or museum

You'll never be grasping for something to talk about with interesting art in front of you. A date at an art gallery will also give each of you insight into the other's likes, dislikes, and more worldly points of view.

Take a tour of a local brewery

As the Pulitzer Prize-winning humorist Dave Barry once said, "Without question, the greatest invention in the history of mankind is beer. Oh, I grant you that the wheel was also a fine invention, but the wheel does not go nearly as well with pizza."

Single Effort learning more about one of life's greatest inventions while sampling flavorful beverages with your date by visiting a local brewery. Afterwards, consider grabbing a slice of pizza (dry cleaning optional!).

Drive out of town for a picnic

Plan a picnic, preferably with a homemade meal and maybe even a nice bottle of wine. Don't have time to make anything at home? Stop by your local grocery store and visit their deli. Many grocery stores have a surprising variety of ready-to-eat picnic-type food at reasonable prices. Don't forget the wine opener along with plates and cups (Zak Designs are perfect for this occasion!).

Attend a comedy show

Laughing together is a great way to build a connection. A comedy show should put you both in a light-hearted and playful mood, so if time permits consider continuing the date with dinner and/or drinks afterwards.

Take a walk in nature

Take a walk through a park, along a nature path, or on a sandy beach. Walking outside in nature will help keep the conversation flowing and give each of you plenty to point out and discuss.

> *Even better, Single Effort the experience by also taking the opportunity to see the world through your date's eyes. Take two cameras (or cell phones) on your walk so you can both take pictures of what you find interesting. After the walk compare photos to determine who's taken the best one. Be sure to save the photos – if your relationship progresses you now have great "first date" memories!*

Sleigh her with romance

Take a sleigh ride in the winter or a hayride in the fall. There are few experiences as romantic as snuggling under a warm blanket and sharing hot cocoa in a horse-drawn sleigh or carriage!

Window shop together

Visit an open-air shopping district and do some window shopping. Shopping with your date can be an intriguing experience – you'll both gain insight into the other's likes and dislikes.

Allow your date to guide you to whatever interests her and expand your horizons outside your comfort zone (that trendy men's clothing store that you never visited – now's your chance!). You might even pick up a unique piece of clothing that you can wear on your next date together. Remember to maintain your Good Knight mindset and open all doors for her!

Volunteer your time

Volunteering is a great way to spend time together while showing your date that you're a thoughtful and caring guy. Check with your city hall or call one of the thousands of not-for-profit agencies out there – like Habitat for Humanity (**www.habitat.org**), Volunteers of America (**www.voa.org**), or your local schools and churches – for volunteer opportunities.

Still having trouble finding a place to volunteer? Look no further than your own neighborhood. Most likely, there's an elderly or shut-in neighbor who could use your assistance. You could rake the leaves from their lawn, shovel snow from their sidewalk, or just bring them a home-cooked meal. Single Effort your First Big Date by helping someone who would be grateful for your assistance.

Stop by a local farm or orchard

Visit a local farm or orchard and pick fresh fruit or vegetables together (apple and cherry picking are great date-friendly activities during the summer and fall in my home state of Michigan). When your baskets are full, consider taking them home and incorporating them into a well-deserved home-cooked meal.

Be an indoor sport

If you both like sporting activities but the weather's not cooperating, consider getting physical with fun indoor activities like bowling, racquetball, laser tag, or indoor ice-skating. If you're both interested in golf, visit an indoor driving range (one of the few places where white tube socks and funny-colored shorts might pass for appropriate dating attire) for some quality tee time together.

Walk the dogs

If you're both pet lovers, Single Effort your date by walking your dogs together. You'll have common interests to talk about and the dogs will enjoy the exercise (and help break the ice, if needed). If there's a pet shop nearby, consider a walking trip to the store for pet snacks – you'll be the talk of Dogtown!

People watch

A favorite casual dating activity. When the weather is nice, find a café with outdoor seating and an unobstructed view of nearby foot traffic. Spend time enjoying your favorite beverages and pleasant conversation. With interesting people passing by, you'll never lack for something to discuss!

Visit the zoo

Just like walking on a nature trail or a sandy beach, you'll be surrounded by interesting things to talk about at the zoo. The animals and scenery make for a topic-rich environment.

Stay active outdoors

Single Effort staying healthy and enjoying your date's company by choosing an outdoor activity. There are hundreds of options that are First Big Date friendly. A few suggestions include kite flying, roller-blading, ice-skating, rock climbing, and mountain biking. Don't forget to pack water and snacks for the both of you!

Build a sandcastle

If you're near a beach, grab some buckets and shovels and visit the shoreline to build a sandcastle together. Don't forget to pack the sunscreen and your favorite beverages. After you're done, make sure you take a picture of your finished creation to share with your date as a remembrance of the time you've spent together.

Build a snowman

If you're in the chilly season and visiting a beach isn't an option, grab the same buckets and shovels and visit a snow-covered plot of land where you can build a snowman together. A local park or your front yard will do nicely. Don't forget to bring something for the snowman's eyes and nose!

Be a Good Knight and make sure your date stays warm. Pack the appropriate gloves and hats – and a thermos filled with hot chocolate – and enjoy the winter day together!

First Date #2 – Locations and Activities to Avoid

There are hundreds, if not thousands, of great places to visit for your First Big Date. However, not all locations and activities will be a good fit. Here are a few that you may want to avoid.

Movie theaters

Most of us enjoy a good movie. But it's often difficult to get to know someone when you're sitting in a darkened theater where talking is frowned upon. Instead, consider renting and watching a movie at home (again, only if she's comfortable visiting you at home – something that needs to be discussed up front). At home, you can pause the movie at any time to continue your conversation or refill her beverage.

Concerts

Most concerts, by design, are quite noisy and unless you're in a suite or a closed room, it can be difficult to hear the other person talking. Save the concert experience for a later date when your relationship has progressed.

Casinos

You want your date night to be light-hearted and fun. When money gets involved it can take the focus away from your date and having a fun time out together. Don't roll craps with your evening – hold onto the dice and visit the casino together when your relationship is further along.

Religious events

People often feel awkward enough attending someone else's religious ceremony, let alone when dating is involved. Even just *talking* about religion can be weighty and will probably not foster the light-hearted conversation your date may be expecting. So unless you're affiliated with the same religious institution, save religious events or ceremonies for later in your relationship.

Major family events and holidays

Your date will probably also feel awkward if you invite her to major family events (weddings, Bar Mitzvahs, or birthday parties) or to a holiday occasion (Thanksgiving, Christmas, etc.) early on in your dating relationship. She most likely won't be comfortable meeting your mother, father, or extended family so soon, and may feel that you're pushing things. Hold off on asking your date to attend major family events and holidays until you've had a chance to get to know one another.

Creative Ideas to Keep the Relationship Magic Flowing

You've progressed through the Mini-Date and the First Big Date, and you're getting along wonderfully – the chemistry is definitely there between you. Congratulations! Don't let up, though – now is not the time to stop having fun (is there ever really a time to stop having fun?!).

Stay creative with your dating experiences and do things together that both of you will enjoy and find exciting. Here are several stimulating "After the First Big Date" ideas to help keep the relationship magic flowing:

Visit a gun range together
If you or your date own a handgun, consider visiting a local gun range. If you don't own a gun, many ranges have guns for rent. Although there's not much opportunity for deep conversation while on the gun range (you both will be wearing ear protection), it can be an intense experience and makes for great conversation afterwards. It's one way to start your date with a real "bang"!

Take a ride in a hot air balloon
Although a hot air balloon ride can be a bit pricey, it's very exhilarating floating up in the air together – definitely an experience neither of you will ever forget. Make sure she's not afraid of heights before you book the ride, however, and remember your camera or cell phone. The views from a hot air balloon are extraordinary and one of a kind!

Get a little dirty

Single Effort helping the environment while spending quality, "dirty" time with your date by planting a tree together. You can wait for Arbor Day (which in the United States is celebrated on the last Friday in April) or simply pick a nice day and plant a sapling where you think one is needed. Plant your tree where it can be visited from time to time so you can see how it's grown – with any luck, just like your relationship!

Croon karaoke

Let your rock star selves shine for the night by crooning karaoke together. Karaoke is a great way to reach outside your comfort zone and share some unique experiences. If you're a bit nervous consider singing a karaoke duet with your date. Having someone by your side should help loosen up those nerves!

Visit a jazz or blues club

Spend an evening at a local music venue. There are few experiences that can compete with sitting back in a jazz or blues club with a martini in hand and a pretty girl at your side. Live music is good for the soul. It energizes and fills your body with a powerful mix of emotions. You'll both feel invigorated by the experience!

Attend a poetry reading

Check out a poetry reading at a local café, club, or bookstore. Or if you're up for it, consider writing a poem together and then reading it to an audience (you can find open mic poetry opportunities in your local event listings). Either way, it's a great opportunity to learn more about the person you're dating while sharing a unique experience.

Visit a senior living complex or a nursing home

Do what you can, together, to brighten the day of residents at a local senior complex or nursing home. Maybe it's planting flowers in a flower box outside the complex or simply sharing a cup of tea and pleasant conversation in the commons area. It's a great feeling to help people who truly appreciate the attention, and it feels twice as good when you share the experience with someone you care about.

"Color in" some time together

Grab a box of crayons and a coloring book and spend time coloring together. There's something therapeutic and relaxing about coloring with crayons. Make sure you post your artwork on the refrigerator and marvel at its beauty. Better yet, take a picture and post it to your Facebook page for the world to see!

Exercise your right brain

Open up to your creative side and consider experiences like clay sculpting, finger painting, or stained-glass artwork. Find a local art shop that's willing to host your experience and have some creative fun together!

Keep fit together!

Sign up to attend a group fitness class together once a week or pencil in a recurring appointment to run side by side on treadmills at your gym. If you prefer the outdoors, find a nature trail in your area and walk or run it together. This is a great way to Single Effort taking care of your health and spending time together on a regular basis.

Take a stroll through a farmer's market

Visit a farmer's market and pick out a basket of eye-catching flowers. Take the flowers home to help liven up each of your living spaces. If time allows, consider also picking up fresh vegetables to take back to your place and use in a home-cooked meal. Then use your cooking skills and wine expertise to wow her with a fantastic feast!

Meet up at a bookstore

Plan a date at a bookstore and find a book that interests both of you. Order coffee or hot chocolate and read through its pages together. Pause often to enjoy the conversation and connection the book stimulates. And if you really enjoy the book, consider purchasing it to continue reading at home together on future dates!

Get progressive with your dinner

Assemble a small group of couples and hold a progressive dinner. In a progressive dinner the couples involved go from home to home enjoying a different course of the meal at each couple's location. For example, if you have four couples in your party, the first couple might serve the appetizer and cocktails, the second would host the soup or salad, the third might create the main course, and the fourth would share a dessert.

A progressive dinner is also a great Single Effort opportunity to introduce your date to friends who may not have met her yet.

Get your game on!

Break out a board game (or two). Stay home and crack open a friendly game of Monopoly, Rummikub, or Yahtzee, along with your favorite snack and beverage. For a unique twist, introduce a game of Mad Libs. Mad Libs is a word game where one person prompts the other for a list of words to substitute for blanks in a story. Then, the other person reads back the story with the new words. Because the person supplying the words has no idea how they'll be used, the stories generated are often quite humorous. This is a great way to get a glimpse of your partner's playful side and gain insight into her point of view on a variety of topics.

Puzzle it out together

Visit a store and select a puzzle that contains several hundred pieces (this will ensure you don't complete it too quickly). Once you get the puzzle home, open up a nice bottle of wine and enjoy a pleasant evening of great conversation while working on the puzzle together.

Hunt for hidden treasures

Get up early and make a morning of visiting garage sales. To maximize your treasure-seeking time, seek out subdivision or neighborhood sales – you can park your car and simply walk from sale to sale. Once your treasure hunting is done, marvel at your new-found riches over a light brunch. Be a Good Knight and don't forget your date's early morning coffee!

Watch the classics

Spend an afternoon watching classic movies. After each of you picks your favorite, watch both movies together in the comfort of your home. She may pick a "chick flick," which is fine – it's good to expand your horizons. But that doesn't mean she shouldn't expand hers as well, so don't shy away from your masculine side! Select a made-for-guys movie that holds particular meaning for you. A few favorites might be *The Shawshank Redemption*, *The Blues Brothers*, *Goodfellas*, or *The Usual Suspects*.

Learn something new together

Get a copy of your local community education flyer and choose a class on a subject the two of you know

nothing about – then attend the class together. Maybe you've always wanted to learn how to speak Italian, maybe she'd like to learn how to perform CPR, or possibly you'd both like to learn sign language. The point is to enjoy time with your date and expand your horizons at the same time – you might be surprised at what you've been missing!

Visit a pool hall

Playing pool works well for all involved. If you know how to play but she doesn't, you'll have fun explaining the rules to her (or vice versa) while you both enjoy the relaxed atmosphere. If neither of you don't know how to play, pool is fun to learn as a couple. There's no pressure to do everything right and you can proceed at your own pace. If you want some tutelage before you try your first game, there are many videos posted on YouTube (**www.youtube.com**) to get you started.

Save a life

*Give blood at a local American Red Cross chapter (**www.redcross.org**). When you're done, treat yourselves to an ice cream at your favorite frozen-goodness establishment. Single Effort helping people in critical need while enjoying your time together.*

Using Technology to Maintain the Connection

In addition to exploring creative ideas for dating, once a relationship starts to blossom it's important that you keep the connection with your date going in between the times you actually see each other.

One way to stay connected is to send short "I'm thinking of you" messages from time to time via email or text. Keep in mind that simpler messages will usually resonate better. The more to the point – while keeping the spark intact – the better.

Here are some charming ways to say "I'm thinking of you" via text message or email:

- Just wanted to say "Hi" and let you know I'm thinking about you!
- Can't wait for our date this weekend…hope you're having a great day!
- Thinking about our last kiss…hoping to see you again soon!
- You were the first thought of my day today!
- I had a great time with you last night…looking forward to many more!

If you're a fan of text messaging you know that being short and sweet is all but a requirement. Here are some even shorter (but still sweet) examples of messages you can send her way:

- TAU (Thinking About You) or TOY (Thinking of You)
- IMU (I Miss You) or MU (Miss You)

- A3 (Anytime, Anyplace, Anywhere – reserved for when you're feeling frisky and your relationship has progressed into physical intimacy)
- IWU (I Want You – also reserved for your more frisky side)
- XO (Kiss and Hug)
- XXX (Kisses – with a naughty bent)

Don't go overboard sending messages. One unsolicited message a day is plenty unless she's given you the green light for more (follow her lead on how many touch points a day is the right amount). If you overwhelm her with messages, you run the risk of becoming an annoyance and souring the relationship.

Revisiting Your Inner Compass

Dating is a lot of fun. It's a blast to go out with different women on a regular basis and explore new activities and locales together. However, keep in mind that dating should not be considered a hobby but rather, a means to an end. What you're really looking for is someone to spend time with on a regular basis, maybe fall in love with, and perhaps spend the rest of your life with. After all, what's the purpose of dating if not to find *the* one for you?

Unfortunately, it's easy to lose sight of the end goal when meeting lots of great women and getting swept up in the excitement and "newness" of it all. To keep yourself on course revisit your inner compass regularly. Pause often to ensure you're still on the right path. As touched upon in chapter 2, your inner compass is your own definition of happiness – let it guide you toward what you seek, not only in life, but also in love.

CHAPTER 12

Success with Online Dating

Most of the discussion so far has revolved around meeting women in person – from working out in a group fitness class, to joining a professional organization, to making the most of a chance encounter at your local grocery store. However, another important method is available, one that casts a much wider net in the female dating pool – this method is online dating.

Online dating uses the Internet and specialized websites to connect men and women with similar likes and interests. There are hundreds of online dating sites, including Match.com (**www.match.com**), eHarmony (**www.charmony.com**), and Plenty of Fish (**www.plentyoffish.com**), to name just a few.

Getting involved in online dating can be exciting but if you're new to the experience, it can also be a little intimidating. I was definitely apprehensive myself. I'm not too proud to say that, when I first signed up on a dating website, I had fears of not getting noticed and even of outright rejection. Would anyone contact me? What if I initiated contact – would she respond? Would I be able to find anyone who had similar interests? Would anyone even take the time to read my profile?

After a few weeks, I happily realized my fears were unfounded. I discovered that if you're moderately proficient at creating a compelling profile (a discussion on how to master the elements of a captivating profile follows later in the chapter) and you can compose brief and light-hearted introductory emails (tips on doing so follow a bit later as well), your chances of meeting new women online are all but certain!

If you're new to online dating, you can think of it as being like diving into an Olympic-size swimming pool filled with Jell-O. You haven't done it before (presumably) but you know it'll be safe – you just need to take the plunge. Indeed, by following a few common-sense tips and techniques, you'll soon be frolicking in an online pool *full* of women – Jell-O optional, of course!

Sitting Idle at Step 2 – A Failed Dating Strategy

Many guys dive into online dating with misguided expectations. They're under the assumption that if they quickly post a profile on a dating website they'll experience a flurry of dating invitations – all of them from great looking women with likes and interests matching theirs.

Their dating strategy looks something like this:

    Step 1. Join a dating website.
    Step 2. <Wait>.
    Step 3. Date beautiful women!

Unfortunately, there are some problems with this approach. Like it or not, you can't just sit idly by once you've joined a dating website and expect the dating offers to come pouring in. Step 2 requires that you invest a little of your time.

After you've created an eye-catching profile, you'll need to get in the habit of visiting your dating site each day to respond to emails and review profiles of potential matches. This isn't a large investment of time by any stretch, but online dating does require some time and effort if you want to be successful.

Your Profile – Two Critical Elements

All online dating websites require that you post information about yourself on the site. You do this in your profile – a little slice of the online dating world reserved just for you. Think of your profile as the heart of who you are on the dating website. It's your homepage and where you let the dating world in on all your best qualities.

Note that your profile is different from your account. An account is something you create so you can log in to a dating website. It contains information on how the dating site should contact you, your billing information, and a few other particulars. Your account is private and personal – not shared with anyone else.

Your profile, on the other hand, is a virtual representation of you for the benefit of other members of the dating site. It's the information about you that you choose to share with others.

An online dating profile is made up of two elements.

1. Your photos
2. Your background

These two elements, common to all dating sites, are critical to your success with online dating. If you don't address them adequately, you may never get the attention you deserve

– allowing other guys to catch the eye of women who should be looking at you.

Remember that on a dating website, women won't have the benefit of talking with you first to discover your charming personality or great sense of humor. They'll have to base their decision on whether or not they want to get to know you solely on the information you provide in your profile via your photos and your background. This is a little like trying to meet women in large group settings (as discussed in chapter 8), only here you can make sure the inner "you" gets equal time by crafting your profile to showcase the things about you that you'd most like women to notice.

Remember too that most women will only spend a few seconds reviewing a guy's profile. If you don't catch their eye in those few seconds, they'll quickly move on to the next candidate. Thus it's in your best interest to spend some time creating a captivating online profile that casts you in the most favorable (but also accurate) light possible. If you post mediocre photos or your background is simply "so-so," you greatly reduce your chances of meeting new women online.

Profile Element #1 – Your Photos

Your photos are the first element critical to your success with online dating. They come in two flavors: primary and secondary. While most dating sites allow you to upload multiple pictures of yourself for your profile, just one of these will appear at the top of your profile and will be visible when a woman is searching for matches or receives match notifications via email. This all-important photo is your primary photo. Your primary photo is similar to your profile picture on Facebook. It's the picture of you that everyone sees first.

The other photos you choose to upload are still important but will only appear after a woman clicks on your profile to learn more about you – these are your secondary photos.

Your primary photo will be a woman's first impression of "you" – and it needs to be a good one! You want to stand out from the crowd of other guys, not merely blend in. If you're serious about online dating, you'll want to take some time to find the best primary photo you can. This may involve sorting through recent photos, seeking the advice of girl+friends, or asking a friend with photography skills to help you out (there are also services that cater to those seeking photos specifically for dating websites – simply search online for "dating photo services").

Here are some Do's and Don'ts to help you put your best face forward in your primary photo:

DO make sure the photo is an accurate representation of you. Resist the temptation to use a picture from 10 years ago when you were 20 pounds slimmer or had more hair. By not posting a current photo of yourself, you'll only set your date, and yourself, up for disappointment later.

DON'T use a group shot as your primary photo – keep the focus on you. You'd be surprised how many men (and women) use a picture with multiple people in the shot as their primary photo. When you do, the obvious question for the women viewing your profile is, "Which one is he?"

DO make sure your primary photo gives a clear view of your face. A front-facing shot is usually best, and you shouldn't be so far back in the photo that no one can see what you look like. Your face and torso should take up most of the picture's real estate.

DON'T use a photo that has you wearing sunglasses or a hat as your primary picture. Women want to see what you look like – not what clothing and fashion accessories you own for your head and face. You can use photos with hats and sunglasses as your secondary photos – sparingly, however.

DO use an image of what you look like on a normal day – not dressed up to the nines on a formal occasion. We all look great dressed up for a night on the town but many women prefer to see the everyday you in a profile picture.

DON'T post a photo that reveals personal information about where you live or work (this applies for any photo – primary or secondary). For example, don't wear a shirt sporting your company logo, and if you post a picture of yourself standing in front of your house, make sure it doesn't reveal where you live (there are some truly bizarre women out there and you don't want one of them showing up on your doorstep unannounced). Also, if you have kids, steer clear of including them in any photos you upload. If you want the women looking at your profile to know you have children, state it in your background.

DO apply the Paparazzi Test.

DON'T use photos where you've cropped other people out of the shot – especially other women. This will only raise questions and foster distrust. For your primary photo, go with a shot of you by yourself. For your secondary photos, it's fine to show other people – as long as you keep everyone in the picture (and get their permission first).

Not a good idea. The obvious question – "Who's that with you?"

*(© Look Better Online at **www.lookbetteronline.com**)*

DO make sure your primary photo is one in which you're smiling. This is *the* most important aspect of a great primary photo. Many studies and surveys have shown that a woman is first drawn to a man's smile – not to how muscular he is or how much hair he has on his head. A good smile is inviting and speaks to a woman, telling her you're confident and fun to be around.

Here's a before and after example of a primary photo. In the "Before" photo you can clearly see the woman's face but that's about it. Her clothing is a bit of a yawn (the jacket isn't helping), she's set too far back in the photo to be seen in any real detail, and although it may be an "everyday" photo, you can see just as much background as you can person. And one other crucial point – she's not smiling.

*The "Before" primary photo –
which can be summarized as "meh."*

(© Look Better Online at **www.lookbetteronline.com**)

And here's the "After" photo with the same girl. Several tips are at work here. The shot is much tighter giving a clear view of her face, she's dressed sharper and is wearing some makeup, and the background is just that – background. But what makes the biggest difference? She's smiling!

*The "After" primary photo – what a difference
a smile and a tighter shot make!*

(© Look Better Online at **www.lookbetteronline.com**)

With secondary photos, the rules become a little less rigid. They should show you having fun and at the same time, give women insight into your personal world. Include some pictures that show you in your true element. Maybe it's tailgating at a football game, hiking in the woods, or doing yard work at home.

Be sure to also incorporate at least one photo that shows your entire body and a couple shots of you with your friends, showing your social side (again, talk to your friends to make sure you have their permission first).

Profile Element #2 – Your Background

The second element of your profile essential to your online dating success is your background. Your background not only gives you the opportunity to put yourself into words but it's also your chance to say, "Hello world – here I am – look at me!"

Depending on the dating website you join, you'll either be prompted to answer questions and your responses will make up your background, you'll write something on your own, or a combination of the two. Your background will contain important data points like your top qualities, what you're looking for in a partner, and some of your distinct likes and dislikes (a detailed breakdown of what your background should contain follows in the next section).

The first version of my background that I wrote was quite lacking. As the saying goes, I didn't know what I didn't know. I simply wrote it like I'd have written a college term paper. I didn't take into consideration a woman's perspective or try to accurately describe my positive attributes, let alone my wants and desires.

In short, it was very impersonal and frankly, just plain dull. The net result? After several days of my profile being posted, not a single woman had contacted me – a bit demoralizing to say the least.

I've since gone through many iterations of my background, based on feedback from women I've met through online dating as well as advice from girl+friends. Their feedback, along with blundering trial and error, eventually paid off. I can now say I've met with success in attracting the type of women I'm interested in online.

A key learning from all my profile missteps is to take into account your audience. Make sure your background is interesting from a woman's point of view. Ask yourself if your introductory paragraph would be compelling to a woman. Would it grab her attention and prompt her to read more?

Then look at your background information as a whole. Do you describe your softer side? (Hint: most women are *not* interested in how much you can bench press or how strong your sex drive is.) Do you express interests you have that many women would also enjoy – examples would be cooking, dancing, or traveling? If you're having difficulty channeling a woman's point of view, consider asking a girl+friend to review what you've written and give you feedback.

Beyond attention to audience, take time to spell and grammar check your background information before posting it for the world to see. Spelling and grammar mistakes in a background can be very costly. They detract from the message you want to convey and could leave your female readers with the impression that you're not very thorough or serious about dating (or very bright, for that matter).

How costly can a spelling mistake be? I'm reminded of a time in my mid-20s when a friend asked me to review his resume. He'd already sent it to a prospective employer, which was unfortunate because I found a typo that had been overlooked. Describing his experience reviewing computational test data, my friend wrote that he had experience "looking for mean shifts." Only problem was, he'd missed the "f" in "shifts." I was laughing so hard I had tears coming out of my eyes as I picked up the phone to call him. I don't know if he got a callback, but hopefully the employer had a good laugh as well!

Mean shifts aside, make sure you also convey a positive attitude in your background. As Winston Churchill once said, "Attitude is a little thing that makes a big difference." No one likes reading why your past relationships didn't work out or why you can't seem to find a compatible date – it ends up coming off as negative and unappealing. Instead, keep the writing in your profile upbeat and positive.

Beyond the basics, here are some tips to help you craft an intriguing background that will attract women:

DO discuss some of your hobbies and the leisure activities you enjoy. If you have many hobbies or interests, pick a few of your favorites to describe – no need to list them all. Try to keep to activities and hobbies that you think will be interesting to your female readers.

DON'T bother describing activities you don't enjoy. Keep an upbeat, positive stance and refrain from reciting events or activities that don't interest you.

DO describe your musical interests. Be as specific as you want to be – you can even list the top two or three songs currently on your phone, iPod, or MP3 player.

DO discuss your career and family aspirations. Do you have kids or want to start a family one day? Or maybe you don't have any desire to have children and wish to pursue your career instead? It's a good idea to let these requirements be known up front to ensure you attract women with similar wants and desires.

DON'T provide your full name, email address, or any other personally identifying information in your background. Just like when posting profile photos, you want to avoid revealing private information in a very public forum.

DO describe a few of your favorite travel adventures and explain why you liked them. Be sure to give some detail and color behind the "why." For example, maybe the sandy beaches of Cancun helped you relax and feel at peace with yourself or you enjoyed feeling like a kid again when visiting Disney World. Some wishful thinking about places you'd like to visit in the future is appropriate as well. Most women love to travel so a colorful description of a likely travel destination will whet their appetite!

DO describe a couple of your favorite foods or dishes. Food is something we all have in common so discussing a favorite food, meal, or restaurant can be a great way to find common interests (unfortunately, "fond" is still not a widely known delicacy!).

DON'T describe your wealth (or lack thereof) or how much you make at your job. You want women to be interested in you – not your money. Money conversations will come in time, with the right relationship. There's no need to put them front and center when trying to meet someone new.

DO remember that humor – being funny and witty – goes a long way in dating (both online and in person). Most women will love to see your humorous side in your profile. Just don't overdo it – you don't want to come across as immature or as a constant jokester.

DO describe the qualities you're seeking in an ideal partner. Do you enjoy philosophical discussions? Would you like to find someone who will make you laugh? Do you prefer someone who enjoys quiet evenings at home playing board games or watching movies? Make it known what qualities and interests you'd like your partner to possess.

By stating what you're looking for you not only attract the women you want to meet, but also filter out women who wouldn't be a good fit. For example, if finding a woman who likes to watch sports is important, then be sure to mention that in your profile. Women who like watching sports will find you appealing and those who find sports a bore won't bother contacting you.

DO be honest and accurate throughout your profile. Gossip can spread fast on a dating website. If you're considered a "player" or someone who isn't forthright in his profile, your odds of garnering new dates diminishes significantly. Keep your background accurate and above board.

DO make sure the length of your profile is appropriate for the dating site you're using. If your background is too short you risk not having enough detail about yourself to capture a woman's attention, too long and women may become bored reading your novel and quickly move on to the next guy's profile. Find your own middle ground (you'll find a convenient "recipe" to build on in the next section).

DON'T be shy or bashful. This is not the time to hold back mentioning your positive traits. Let everyone know why you're a great catch!

The very *best* advice in crafting a compelling background, however, comes from Oscar Wilde – the great 19th-century writer and arbiter of taste – who summed it up in just a few words: "Be yourself; everyone else is taken."

Recipe for a Compelling Background

To create a compelling background, focus on putting together five short paragraphs that describe the essence of who you are (a real-world example follows). Even if you use a site like eHarmony that asks you to answer questions to create your profile, the breakdown here will still be helpful as many of the same topics will be addressed.

Section One – Introducing You

This section is the most important part of your background. If you don't craft an interesting introduction, your female audience won't read any further and will simply move on to the next guy. Start out by telling your reader a little bit about yourself and what you're looking for in an ideal partner.

Keep this section short and sweet – no more than three or four sentences. Make it enjoyable and of course, personal. Refrain from using quotes from movies, songs, or poems, and stay clear of weighty technical jargon and complicated words.

This section is also an opportunity to filter out women you don't want to meet. For example, if you're not interested in meeting anyone who can't gargle the theme to Star Wars using your favorite beverage (you never know, it doesn't hurt to ask), make this clear to your female readers up front!

Section Two – Your Top Qualities

Next, describe yourself in a bit more detail. This is the section where you talk about your positive qualities and interests in a way that doesn't come across as arrogant or egotistical yet still projects confidence.

Remember, the crucial difference between confidence and arrogance is intent. If your intent is to impress your reader with how smart or important you are, what you're saying will come across as arrogant. Instead, focus on presenting your top qualities and interests with some levity and flair.

Finally, feel free to discuss not just the types of activities you enjoy, but also the adventures and experiences a woman might expect if she were dating you.

If there's any section of your background where girl+friend assistance would be helpful, it would be this one – use the advice of your girl+friends to make sure you've painted an interesting picture of yourself without sliding into self-importance.

Section Three – Your Partner Request

In the third section, go into more detail about what you're looking for in a female companion. Be realistic here but at the same time, be honest and keep to your standards. If you absolutely require someone of the same religious faith or maybe someone who's shorter than you in height (we all have our own unique requirements), then mention it in this section.

Don't shoot for the moon. Chances are slim that you're going to find a woman who was a recent winner in your state's beauty pageant and also loves to watch Monday Night Football while discussing stock car racing during the commercial breaks.

Be as honest as possible, though, about what you're looking for. That way, when you do have someone contact you, she'll be much more likely to fit the bill.

Section Four – Partner and Relationship Underline

The second-to-last section of your background is your chance to underline, or reinforce, one or two of the key qualities you're looking for in an ideal relationship. Keep this section short and to the point.

Section Five – Closing

This is the last thing a woman is going to read about you, so make it compelling and memorable. Try to stay away from clichéd and over-used phrases and come up with something brief and unique – a closing that would leave even George Costanza intrigued and wanting to learn more!

A Sample Background

Here's a real-world example you can use to jump-start the creation of your own background. It incorporates many of the tips and recommendations already discussed.

Intro – Make it enticing and easy to understand.
I'm a professional in the technology field and newly single. I'm confident, intelligent, and easy going, and I'm looking for someone who likes to laugh and isn't shy to speak her mind. If we connect and the chemistry is there, I'd love to see where it goes!

Top Qualities – Don't be shy here. List some of your best qualities.

I like to have fun, keep myself in great shape, and I'm a gentleman at heart. I enjoy all aspects of being with the right person – we could be spending the evening together cooking dinner and sharing a nice bottle of wine, out at a local restaurant enjoying our conversation, traveling to our next adventure in another country, or dancing the night away at a club. It's the "who" I'm with that's much more important to me than "what" we are doing – with the right person, the sky's the limit!

Partner Request – List the key qualities you're looking for in a partner.

I'm looking for someone who's intelligent, witty, good looking (with a great smile), knows what she wants, and is family oriented. I love discussions that are challenging and make us both reflect on the topic at hand, so a good conversationalist is important, too! I'm not looking for long-distance relationships, however – I'm only interested in meeting women local to me in Michigan (sorry).

Partner and Relationship Underline – Reinforce a couple of the main qualities you're looking for.

I value open and honest communication and I'm looking for a relationship that is just that – honest and trusting and filled with passion!

Closing – Make it memorable!

I'm looking for someone to share in life's thrills – naughty and nice! Someone with a spark in her eye and a killer smile. Are you the one?

After posting your background, revisit it regularly to update it with any new information you'd like to share (but remember to watch the mean shifts!). It could be new places you've visited, recent books you've read, or simply new song additions to your music library. Let your female readers know you have many interests and like to stay active!

Capturing Her Attention with Your Introductory Email

Once your profile is in place, you have two options. Option one is to sit back and wait for women to find your profile (i.e. "Sitting Idle at Step 2"). That *might* work. The second option, however, dramatically increases your odds – it involves initiating contact with women you find intriguing.

A well-rounded online strategy will involve both options: sitting back and waiting after you've posted a well-crafted profile – letting women who are a bit more proactive find you online – and also taking the initiative to do some searching yourself – seeking out women who meet your particular criteria.

Because the desire to meet people with comparable interests is one of the main reasons people turn to online dating, most dating websites give you the ability to search for women with similar interests. Once found, you can send them email through the website's email system (after a while you'll probably realize that, for a variety of reasons, it's a bit of a pain to use the email system on a dating website – the next chapter contains some guidance as to when it might be appropriate to use your personal email address instead).

One note of caution when communicating with women on a dating website – many sites have a feature called "winking" (or something similar like an "ice breaker" option) that allows you to send an "I noticed you" message to a woman without expending any real effort – like winking at someone from across the room. You may be tempted, but don't wink – it lowers your chances of success.

Because sending a wink is so easy, it's gotten out of hand. Many women get inundated with winks and as a result, simply ignore them altogether, focusing instead on the guys who take the time to send them a nicely worded email. So if you want to get noticed, don't be a wuss – skip the wink and send an email!

To help your message stand out from the flood of emails women receive daily on dating websites, you need to craft something that will grab their attention – something that's both compelling and unique yet still casts you in an approachable light. Your introductory email message should be brief, respectful, and light-hearted. At the same time it should contain enough substance to compel a woman to read your profile and respond back to you.

To weave together a compelling introductory email, just remember three guidelines and one common thread. The three guidelines are:

1. Create an intriguing subject line
2. Personalize the body
3. Wrap it up with a relevant question

And the common thread between the three guidelines? Use snippets of *her* background in each part of your message.

The first part of a compelling email message is the subject line. And just like your primary photo, it needs to be captivating! When sending an email to a woman you've never met or talked with, an eye-catching subject line will be the most important element in grabbing her attention. If you don't have something interesting to say in the subject of your email, your message will probably not be read.

According to several women I've dated, it's not uncommon to receive between 10 and 20 emails a day from guys looking to start an online conversation. To compound the issue, most dating websites only preview the subject line of the emails sitting in a member's Inbox – the content of the email is only revealed when the message is opened by the recipient.

The Inbox for a typical woman on a dating website (names redacted)

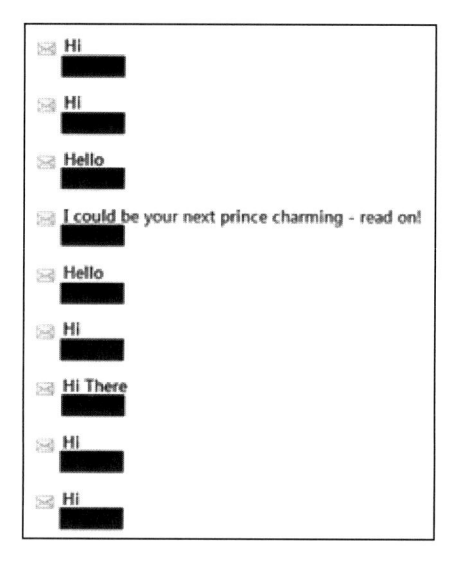

![Inbox screenshot showing subject lines: Hi, Hi, Hello, I could be your next prince charming - read on!, Hello, Hi, Hi There, Hi, Hi]

(© *Single Effort. Image courtesy of the author.*)

If you're a woman who hasn't logged into your dating site in a few days and you're now staring at 99 emails all with "Hi" or "Hello" as the subject line and one that says "I could be your next prince charming – read on!" which one are you going to open first?

An intriguing subject line gives a woman a reason to open your message. It can be crafted in a variety of ways. One technique is to use catchy phrases like "Don't read this, unless…" or famous one-liners from movies like "Of all the gin joints in all the towns in all the world, you walk into mine."

Another method that works very well (and will be *the* best method for many women) is to mention something you've read in her background. This will set you apart from all the guys who send the same message to every woman they contact and will show a woman you have a genuine interest in what she has to offer.

For example, if a woman's background states that she likes reading and has young children, create a subject line that ties those facts together to grab her attention. "Harold and the Purple Crayon is one of my favorites!" is definitely a subject line that will stand out from the bevy of others already in her Inbox.

Whatever your approach, be sure to catch the eye of the woman you're interested in with an intriguing subject line. Entice her into reading your email and taking the next step toward learning more about you!

The second part of a compelling introductory email is what you write in the body of your message. It should be brief and personalized to her background. Start by introducing yourself and then reference a piece of information (or two) from her background.

As an example, let's assume a guy wants to email a woman whose background states that she likes wine and enjoys traveling. We'll compare two emails from the same hypothetical guy to the same woman – the only difference being the personalization factor. The first is composed using the traditional "email factory" method, recycling the same message, over and over again, without any regard to personalization.

We'll call this version "Opportunity Lost":

Hi,

I read your profile and you look really cute! Please take a look at my profile and if you like what you see, please email me back!

Joe

Believe it or not, this example is *very* typical of the type of introductory message that women receive on dating websites. If you simply add a little personalization to the emails you send – just a little – you'll be ahead of 90% of the other guys in the online dating world vying for the same relationship opportunities.

Contrast the first version with this one, which we'll call "So Much Better It's Not Even Close":

Hi there,

I read through your profile and you definitely sound like someone who appreciates good wine! I also enjoy wine and travel and would love to pair the two for a trip to France one day – visiting local wineries and sampling their wines. Do you have a favorite wine?

I would like to get to know you more. Please email me back if you're interested in talking.

Joe

By weaving a woman's background into your email you demonstrate genuine interest – showing that you've actually taken the time to read through what she posted and that you aren't spamming her with a form letter that's already gone out to a hundred other women. Your reader will appreciate the individual attention you've paid her and you'll be much more likely to receive a positive response.

Finally, at or near the end of your message, ask a relevant question. This is the third and final part of creating an effective email. It makes it easy for the woman you're contacting to know how to respond. Here again, personalization is key – take into account the information contained in her background in creating your question.

Many times a guy will write a great introductory email, the woman will read the email, but then she won't have a clear idea of how to respond back. Or she may simply be shy and unsure of how to phrase her response. In either case, this could cause her to delay responding or worse yet, not respond at all. The same philosophy mentioned in chapter 9 holds true here – by asking a question you lower any barriers there may be to a continued conversation. You make it easy for her to see how she can respond back to you.

Suppose the woman you're interested in mentioned that she likes mountain biking in her background. You could use that information in closing your email: "I love mountain biking too! Do you have a favorite biking trail?"

To sum up, as you work to craft an introductory email that will get you noticed, keep in mind three straightforward pointers:

1. Create an interesting subject line – entice her into reading more about you
2. Personalize the body to her background – stay away from form letters
3. Wrap it up with a relevant question – lower any barriers for her to respond back to you

And one last point – as touched on in chapter 11, don't go overboard with your emails. Send only one introductory message to each woman you want to meet and then wait for a response. If you try to rush things by sending more than one email before you receive a response, you may come across as desperate – and never hear back from her.

Always wait for a response before sending further emails, and if you don't get a response? So long! So what? Move on. Find some lemons, grab a drink, and make your own party!

A Sample Introductory Email

Here's a real-world example of an introductory email to help pull it all together:

A personalized subject line that will get you noticed.
Subject: Lobster…Yummers!

In her background she mentioned that traveling was a key interest of hers.
Hi,
I read your profile and you sound like someone I'd like to get to know. I love traveling as well – the most interesting place I've visited to date is Shanghai, China.

She also mentioned that she valued family.
A bit about me…I'm intelligent, stay in shape, love a great conversation, and I'm a romantic at heart. I'm very outgoing and happy – and I'm looking to share that happiness with the right person. Family is also very important to me.

Again tying into her background and closing with a question.

You mentioned traveling to Maine — I love Maine lobster! Do you have any favorite restaurants in Maine?

CHAPTER 13

Continuing Adventures in Online Dating

As you continue your journey down the online dating trail, you'll experience a wide variety of adventures. Some dates will go exceedingly well. Others, maybe not so much. One thing is certain, however – you'll definitely meet and date a lot of interesting women, in the end hopefully finding *the* one for you!

In exploring the world of online dating, you're sure to come upon areas that aren't well marked. To keep from wandering off the path and into a dating sink hole, you'll want to consider, in advance, some likely pitfalls and decisions that you may encounter.

Should you trust someone you've met online with your email address and phone number? Once you've gotten started dating, do you date one woman exclusively or is it better to date several? And how do you keep it all straight between them if you're dating more than one woman at the same time?

Fear not, intrepid online traveler! Single Effort tips to keep you on the straight and narrow follow here. They'll guide you around any obstacles you may encounter, help keep you happy on the trail, and improve your chances of finding what you seek!

Your Personal Info (The Orange Peel Consideration)

Correspondence is a common denominator for screening and dating the women you meet online. With someone you've just met, a typical progression is to start conversing through the dating site's email system and then, over time, to begin using either your phone or a personal email address (or both).

Using the dating site's email system has several benefits. One is that it makes searching prior correspondence easy – your communication is all in one place, so looking up what you said when to whom is a simple matter.

Another benefit is that it allows you to keep your personal email address and phone number private. There are always a few women prowling dating sites trying to scam guys for their money and others who may be a few feathers short of a whole duck. So it's probably best *not* to share your personal email address or phone number right out of the gate.

However, sometimes it'll be cumbersome to stay in contact through your dating site's email system – your computer may not be handy, and using personal email or text message via your phone may seem a whole lot easier. If you find yourself with a few minutes to kill and want to send a quick message (e.g. waiting in a long checkout line at the store), it's usually easier to do so through your phone using a personal email account rather than navigating the dating site.

You may also find that email (regardless of the system it originated from) can be a bit impersonal. As your comfort level increases, you may yearn for a phone conversation with someone you've met online.

To make it easier, and a bit more personal, to keep in contact with the women you meet on dating websites, consider giving out your personal email address and/or phone number when you feel like you've formed a connection and a mutual feeling of trust has been established.

However, if you want to add an additional layer of protection as you make the leap to personal email, you can use a disposable email address at first (many guys – and numerous women – do this as a matter of course in online dating). A disposable email address (also called an "alias") is an alternate address you create through your email provider. It lets you send and receive email from and to your main account without anyone knowing your primary address. And when you're done with this disposable address, you just turn it off – ensuring future messages sent to it won't land in your Inbox.

How will you know when to step outside the "safe" world of your dating website's email system? Unfortunately, there isn't a "one size fits all" rule. It's actually quite subjective – it's up to you to decide when the time is right.

If you'd like help making this determination, food can be a good litmus test. We all have different levels of tolerance for who or what we allow to come in contact with our food. You can leverage your own "food touchiness" to determine whether or not it's a good time to relinquish your personal information – a method I call the "Orange Peel Consideration."

Simply ask yourself this question: "Would I be comfortable handing the woman in question an orange and walking away – letting her peel it out of my view – and then returning a few minutes later and eating it?"

If the answer is a resounding "Yes!" then you're in the citrus zone and good to go! If the answer is a "No" or a "Maybe," consider walking the orange grove with her a bit more – conversing through the dating site's email system until your comfort level is reached.

The Orange Peel Consideration takes two factors into account – trust and subjectivity. Trust is in play because even though you don't understand the ins and outs of her personal hygiene yet (presumably you'll gain some insight into that down the road if she's a keeper), you're at least convinced she'd handle your food in a clean and safe manner. When it comes to trusting someone, this can be a safe enough starting point – as Ernest Hemingway so eloquently put it, "The best way to find out if you can trust somebody is to trust them."

Because each person has different standards when it comes to food (and trust), this approach also provides a window into your own subjectivity. We all have different thresholds in such matters – the Orange Peel Consideration will simply highlight your current subjective impression so that you can make the final call.

Dating Multiple Women (Variety Is the Spice of Life)

As you become familiar with the online dating experience, you'll eventually come to a point where you'll have to make a decision about how many women to date at the same time (not a bad decision to have to make!).

One option is what many call "serial dating." It means you're seeing the same woman (and no others) until you break it off with her. Serial (or one-at-a-time) dating is very common and a widely accepted dating practice.

There are, of course, some benefits to serial dating. For one, it has the potential to allow for a deeper relationship – especially if the woman you're dating feels the same way and also wants to date you exclusively (which is actually rare early in an online relationship). In addition, it makes keeping track of your date's likes and dislikes much easier since she's the only one you're seeing.

The downsides of serial dating, however, usually outweigh the benefits. When you limit yourself to dating one woman you can miss out on meeting other potentially great women. You're also obliged to follow *her* schedule. If you want to go out on a date on a Friday night and she's not available, you're out of luck.

Another downside (and this one's a biggie) is that your dating "value" could be lowered if you stick to one woman. Like it or not, dating follows the principle of supply and demand. That which is in high demand we often deem more valuable than that which is in low demand. By dating more than one woman at a time you're more likely to be seen as someone who is "in demand" and thus be more appealing (and desirable) in a dating relationship.

The second option is to date multiple women. An upside to this approach is that it gives you a backup plan in case of unforeseen events. For example, if your date cancels at the last minute you'll most likely have a "Plan B" available so you won't have to waste those expensive theater tickets.

Also, dating multiple women will afford you some diversity. As the saying goes, variety is the spice of life. If one date is fun to go karaoking with, another may offer intellectual stimulation and deep conversation, and a third could be the sensuous one you take dancing. It's fun to have a varied mix of qualities in the women you date until you can find someone who encapsulates all the qualities you're looking for. However, when dating multiple women you'll need to keep a keen focus on your calendar to prevent double booking conflicts.

If you see yourself as more of a "one woman at a time" kind of guy, feel free to follow your own compass. Though dating multiple women certainly has its benefits, nothing says you have to. Some guys will choose to communicate with multiple women in the very early stages of the online dating process (as you progress through getting-to-know-you emails and your first or second date), and then stick to serial dating as things get more serious. If this is the approach that works best for you, go for it!

While dating multiple women can be great, there is, of course, an important exception to when it's appropriate, and that's if you believe a woman you're seeing is the one for you. In that case, dating her exclusively is the recommended course of action. You don't want to look like you're "playing the field" – and risk alienating her – if you feel a strong connection.

If you haven't yet found the one though and you decide to date multiple women, keep in mind the Golden Rule. Be up front early on in your dating relationships – let each woman know you're dating other women as well.

One final note – when you date multiple women it can be easy to go overboard and date too many at the same time. So be sure to keep the churn of new women to a reasonable level. Each new woman you meet and date will represent a commitment of both your time and your money. If you're constantly dating someone new you'll find it can get expensive quickly.

A nice evening out for two on a First Big Date, like dinner at an up-scale restaurant, could run over $100. And it'll probably consume your entire evening as you work on getting to know each other. Go out on several First Big Dates a month with new acquaintances you've met online and it quickly adds up. What you spend on getting-to-know-you dates for a month could easily amount to a car payment!

Instead of meeting someone new each week, try balancing quality vs. quantity. If you've found two or three women you're interested in, consider investing the time to get to know them first before you start dating a pool of other women. As you get to know them, your dates can become less costly as you transition into activities that involve spending time at home together or where you split the cost.

Keeping Track of the Details

Even if you're only dating two or three women it can still be challenging to remember the important details for each one – from likes and dislikes, to hobbies and passions, to notable points you've discussed in prior conversations. Remembering the details of prior emails and conversations is important as you get to know your date better – it lets her know you're paying attention to what she's told you and will help you keep your conversation more focused and personal.

Unfortunately, many guys (myself included), have a difficult time remembering the important details concerning one woman, let alone two, three, or even four. Once one thing goes in something else must come out – like a never-ending game of Whac-A-Mole.

To keep track of all the pertinent information regarding the women you're meeting through online dating (as well as women you meet outside dating websites), consider writing everything down where it can be easily referenced. This could be as simple as writing notes to yourself on paper or on your smartphone, or as elaborate as using a spreadsheet on your computer or a mobile note taking solution like the popular Evernote application (**www.evernote.com**).

And finally, one other technique to help you remember details about the women you're talking with (and dating) is to use visual cues. If your phone allows, attach a photo taken from the dating website to each woman's phone number stored in your phone. Then, when she calls, her photo will appear and should jog your memory – helping you recall important details before your conversation starts. This comes in especially handy when you're dating two women with the same first name!

Whatever method you choose, consider adopting a system to keep track of each woman's status and prior discussion points. When you get a chance, use your notes as a refresher before starting a new conversation with someone you've already talked with. You'll resonate much more with her if you can refer to topics and facts that have come up in previous conversations.

Thanks, But No Thanks...Revisited

If you're on a dating website long enough, you're going to get your share of women contacting you who you don't want to pursue a relationship with. It could be that you don't find any common interests in a woman's background, you don't like how she appears in her photos, or possibly there isn't enough information in her profile to generate interest on your part.

As enticing as someone's background may be, stay away from anyone who hasn't posted a photo of herself. If a woman hasn't taken a few minutes to post a photo, she probably isn't serious about dating, lacks self-esteem, or quite simply, is unattractive – none of which are great options. If no photo is present: *Unray wayaay uicklyqay!*

For women who've contacted you on a dating website but haven't managed to spark your interest – here too you should follow the Golden Rule. Don't leave them waiting for a response (you would certainly want the same courtesy). Just as you would following a Mini-Date where the chemistry didn't develop, send a short "Thanks, but no thanks" email that lets the woman know you appreciate her contacting you but don't have any interest in pursuing further dialogue.

Here are a few gentle (and succinct) ways to say "No thank you" to women who've initiated contact with you through a dating website:

- Thank you for your email. I'm flattered that you chose to contact me but I'm not interested. Good luck in your search!

- Thanks so much for the email but based on our profiles I don't think we have enough in common. You sound like a great catch – I'm sure you'll find Mr. Right soon!

- I appreciate the offer to talk via phone. You list many wonderful qualities in your profile but I don't think that we're a good match. I'm sure you'll find the right person for you – good luck in your search!

CHAPTER 14

And Then, She Kissed Me...

Looking back on the time after I realized my marriage was over, I remember one song helping me keep everything in perspective. "If Today Was Your Last Day" by the band Nickelback reinforced my conviction that the new life ahead of me could be even better than the one I was leaving behind.

It begins with the following lyrics:

> *My best friend gave me the best advice*
> *He said each day's a gift and not a given right*
> *Leave no stone unturned, leave your fears behind*
> *And try to take the path less traveled by*
> *That first step you take is the longest stride*
>
> *If today was your last day*
> *And tomorrow was too late*
> *Could you say goodbye to yesterday*
> *Would you live each moment like your last*
> *Leave old pictures in the past*
> *Donate every dime you have*
> *If today was your last day*

In your single life, try to live by what Nickelback's song expresses so eloquently – leave no stone unturned and leave your fears behind. Take the path less traveled and do your best to live each moment as if it were your last. As you travel the single path, keep your eyes open to new experiences – and if you're looking with an open heart, you'll eventually find the right someone for you.

As I walked my own path as a single guy, I found that I was quite happy – but every now and then, also a bit sad. Happy because I was having a great deal of fun living life to its fullest, but sometimes a bit sad too thinking, "Would I ever find the one for me?"

One night, on a first date with a woman I'd just met online a few days prior, I felt butterflies in my stomach when her eyes met mine. We had a connection that night that I can't describe in words – it was as if we had known each other for many lifetimes.

We talked for hours and during our conversation I realized a strange feeling had come over me – a feeling I'd never experienced before. Like a gentle tug when picking a beautiful flower, something was pulling on my heart strings. I thought to myself, "Could she be the one for me?"

And then, she kissed me...

Glossary

background – One of two core elements in your profile on a dating website (see profile). The other is your photos – primary and secondary. Your background is the description of you that is shared with other members of the dating site. To garner the right attention, it needs to be well written and enticing (so seek help from girl+friends and watch the mean shifts!).

BBB – Short for Bed Bath & Beyond. This home goods store is a mainstay for single guys furnishing their own place. BBB coupons are valuable and never expire, so save them up for a purchase palooza!

Call the ball – A U.S. Navy communication sent by the control tower to an aircraft pilot. It refers to the pilot sighting the "ball," or light, on the deck of a carrier that lets him know he's on the correct flight path for landing his plane. As a single guy, you too need to "Call the ball" to ensure you're on the right approach when talking with women you meet in chance encounters.

caramelize (cooking) – To heat a food to the point that its sugar proteins begin to turn brown and produce a caramel flavor. Must be done at relatively high temperatures – typically 300 degrees F or higher.

Chicken Fingers Standard – A helpful standard designed to ensure that your first date, or Mini-Date, with a woman is appropriately inexpensive and easy to leave if the chemistry isn't right. When planning your Mini-Date, stick to activities (like going out for chicken fingers) that cost under $10. While actually buying chicken fingers for your date is *not* recommended, your Mini-Date should be almost as inexpensive!

chivalry – A term born of the medieval institution of knighthood incorporating gallantry, courtesy, and honor, or the qualities of an ideal knight. Today, chivalry is meant to convey consideration and respect for women. It forms the cornerstone of a Good Knight mindset (see Good Knight).

chop (cooking) – To cut a food into small pieces, roughly ¼-inch chunks. Often compared with minced and diced – chopped is the largest of the three cuts (remember, "minced, diced, and chopped" or "small, medium, and large" – where "large" still means fairly small!).

Costco Effect – The quality of never being the same experience twice. Like walking through a Costco or Sam's Club, there's something new to see, taste, and explore each time you visit. The world of wine exhibits the Costco Effect – lucky are those who can visit often!

dating kit – A small (and discreet) set of items placed in a bag or pouch and stored in your vehicle's console or glove box. Its purpose is to prepare you for the unexpected, to help you avoid potentially embarrassing situations, and to give you a leg up on ensuring your date is successful. A dating kit generally consists of breath fresheners, a single-use toothbrush, condoms, and a compliment (to be given to your date!).

deglazing (cooking) – Removing the sticky bits of roasted goodness left on the bottom of a frying pan with the help of a liquid. Typically done with wine over high heat. The sauce resulting from the deglazing process is called "fond" (see below).

dice (cooking) – To cut a food into smaller pieces than when chopping (see chop). Often compared with minced and chopped – diced is the middle size of the three cuts (remember, "minced, diced, and chopped" or "small, medium, and large").

First Big Date – Your second date with a woman, to be scheduled only after a successful Mini-Date (meaning there's enough chemistry and interest for another get-together). This is your chance to do something special that will stand out prominently from other dates a woman has already had and hopefully pique her interest in future outings.

fond (cooking) – The sauce resulting from deglazing (see above). Fond is so rich in flavor it should be added to the official list of delicacies (if such a list exists!).

George's Ten-Minute Rule – Named for George Costanza, this rule holds that you should spend no more than ten minutes talking to someone you've just met in a chance encounter. This forces you to be succinct and to the point – and leave her wanting more!

girl+friend – Someone who is a girl plus a good friend, but there is no romance involved. Compare with "girlfriend" (where romance is definitely involved!). From creating a female-friendly home to building a stellar profile on a dating website, girl+friends (because they're women) can help single guys in myriad ways when it comes to attracting the opposite sex.

Good Knight – A persona to emulate as a single guy (and beyond!). Based on the medieval concept of chivalry, Good Knight behavior is a sure-fire way to impress women on dates or in chance encounters (see chivalry). Good Knight behavior includes, but is not limited to, opening a door for a woman, pulling out and pushing in your date's chair at dinner, and ensuring she gets home safely after your date concludes.

Grocery Cart Effect – A phenomenon that works in your favor when you start a conversation with a woman who's pushing a grocery cart. The cart acts as an indirect barrier between you, giving her a sense of security and comfort that makes it easier for her to open up to a chance conversation.

Inverse Cleaning Theory of Hotness – A theory that holds that the cleaning ability of a housekeeper is inversely proportional to her attractiveness. That is, as a woman's "hotness" goes up, her cleaning ability declines. Controversial? Yes. Accurate? Usually.

KISS – Keep It Simple, Stupid! Useful advice in a host of situations and the secret to striking up a conversation with a woman you've just met. Never over-think things – if you're unsure what to do, KISS!

mean shifts (as in "Watch the mean shifts!") – The little details that can throw you off when you're trying to make a great impression on a woman through your writing. Mean shifts include spelling, grammar, or any kind of careless mistake. They're especially important when developing your online dating background and conversing with women via email. The term originates from a misspelling found in a resume where the "f" in "shifts" was mistakenly omitted!

mince (cooking) – To cut a food into *very* small pieces. Often compared with diced and chopped – minced is the smallest of the three cuts (remember, "minced, diced, and chopped" or "small, medium, and large").

Mini-Date – Your first date with someone new. Usually held at a location that's inexpensive and not time intensive so you can avoid spending a lot of money and leave early if needed. When planning your Mini-Dates, try to adhere to the Chicken Fingers Standard (see above).

mise en place – Pronounced "meez ahn plahs." A French expression that means "putting into place" or "all in place." It's the act of having all the ingredients for a meal prepared and at hand, in a well-organized fashion, *before* you start to cook. Trust me – this will save you some major headaches!

Orange Peel Consideration – A method to help you gauge how much personal information (phone number, email address, etc.) to share with someone you've met online. Based on your "food touchiness," the Orange Peel Consideration highlights your current level of trust with someone new.

Paparazzi Test – A rule of thumb to help you decide whether your current dress and grooming are acceptable for public consumption (because you never know when you're going to meet someone you'd like to get to know better!). In a nutshell, it involves gauging whether you'd be comfortable having your look captured by paparazzi and posted on the cover of a tabloid. If the outfit you're sporting passes the Paparazzi Test, you're good to go!

primary photo – Your main photo on a dating website. It anchors your online profile and appears when a woman searches for matches or receives match notifications via email. This is a woman's first impression of "you" so make it good!

profile – A little slice of the online dating world reserved just for you. You can think of it as your dating "homepage," where you let women in on all your best qualities. Your profile is made up of two core elements: your photos (primary and secondary) and your background (see primary photo, secondary photos, and background).

sauté (cooking) – To brown a food quickly by moving it around over fairly high heat in a small amount of oil or butter – much like when stir frying. Used for food that's already in smallish pieces or has been cut into pieces. "Sauté" literally means "to jump," so keep those food pieces jumping!

sear (cooking) – To brown quickly over high heat, keeping the food in one place until it forms a crust on the surface – in contrast to browning or sautéing where the food is moved around quickly in the pan.

secondary photos – On a dating website, photos that are hidden until someone opens your profile and clicks through them. Your profile will usually have many secondary photos, but only one primary photo (see above).

Single Effort – Working smart, maximizing your time, and multiplying your outcomes as a single guy. An example would be keeping in shape while at the same time meeting new women by attending a female-friendly exercise class. Single Effort is also about *making an effort* as a single guy – being proactive and not waiting for someone to come knocking at your door. It's about charting your own course and living a fulfilling life.

Sitting Idle at Step 2 – A (flawed) strategy followed by many guys when it comes to online dating. It goes something like this:
    Step 1. Join a dating website.
    Step 2. <Wait>.
    Step 3. Date beautiful women!
In reality, you can't just sit back in Step 2 and expect the dating offers to come pouring in. You've got to invest a little of your time!

So long! So what? Move on. – She's simply not interested. So what? Move on! No matter how hard you try there are just some women who will not be interested in you. However, there are hundreds if not thousands more to meet, so get out there!

squashed grapes – Wine ☺.

Unray wayaay uicklyqay! – Code for "Run away quickly!"

wine – An alcoholic beverage made from fermented grapes and grape juice (see squashed grapes). Many women are captivated by a guy who understands the basics of this simple but infinitely complex beverage. Brush up on your wining skills and watch the ladies swoon!

wink or winking – A way of sending an "I noticed you" poke or ping on dating websites without expending any real effort. Many women get inundated with winks and as a result, simply ignore them altogether, focusing instead on guys who take the time to send a nicely worded email. Don't be a wuss – skip the wink and send an email!

INDEX

Page numbers with an italicized "i" refer to illustrations.

A
Amazon.com, "Amazon Prime" membership, 32
Appearance
    chart, A color-matching table for a single guy's wardrobe, 162
    clothing, appropriate to event, 160–161
    footwear and shoes, 161–163
    meeting women, and, 159–161
    "Paparazzi Test", 160
    personal grooming, hair, 163–165
    shoes and socks, coordinating, 162–163
Articles and books, recommended
    "How Humans Cognitively Manage an Abundance of Mate Options" (Lenton and Francesconi), 148
    "How Much Will My Divorce Cost?" (Meyer), 15
    Wine for Dummies (McCarthy and Ewing-Mulligan), 145
Attorneys
    cost factors, 15
    divorce and, 14
    vs. divorce mediators, 13

B
Background, defined, 255
Barry, Dave, about beer, 200
BBB (Bed Bath & Beyond)
    coupons, 33
    single-guy friendly, 33
Böll, Heinrich, "How Much is Enough?", 26
Bucket List, creating, 21–22

C
"Call the ball", defined, 255
Caramelize (cooking), defined, 255
Carlin, George, about de-cluttering and downsizing, 27
Cell phones. *See* Technology
Chemistry
    absence of, 230–231
    dating, 175, 191–192, 193, 194, 199
    helpful quotations, 173
    meeting women, 172
    online dating, 250–251
"Chicken Fingers Standard"
    dating and, 192–193
    defined, 255
Chivalry
    aspects of, 6, 177
    benefits of, 177–179
    defined, 256
    specific examples of, 176

Chop (cooking), defined, 256
Churchill, Winston, about attitude, 227
Cleaning products. *See* Products, cleaning
Cooking
   appliances, tools and utensils, 87
   cooking ability, importance of, 81
   cooking oil, olive vs. vegetable, 93–94
   cooking oil, testing temperature, 94
   cooking oil, types, 92
   deglazing, 115–116, 116i
   garlic, 95
   high heat vs. low heat, 90–91
   ingredients, essential, 91
   ingredients, gathering, 85
   kitchen hygiene, 104–105
   magazines, 82
   mincing, dicing, and chopping, 98, 98i
   mise en place, 85
   onions, 96–98
   peppercorns vs. table pepper, 99
   pots and pans, non-stick vs. stainless steel, 87–91
   pots and pans, pizza pans, 122
   recipe sources, 105, 116
   resources for learning about, 82
   salt and pepper, types, 99
   sautéing, 97
   searing, 94
   seasoning, salt and pepper, 101
   television networks and programs, 82
   using fresh ingredients, 84
   wine, use in cooking, 116–117
"Costco Effect", defined, 130, 256
Counseling
   benefits of, 10, 11
   individual counseling, 10, 11
   marriage counseling, 10

D

Date Night Checklist
   dating, 60
   downloads, 60
   living space, 60
   worksheets and forms, 60
Dating
   See also Online Dating
   anticipating your date's wishes, 74
   "batting average", 198
   big dates, 199
   big dates, activities to avoid, 205–206
   big dates, recommended activities, 199–205, 207–213
   body language, interpreting, 194–195

chemistry, 175, 191–192, 193, 194, 199
"Chicken Fingers Standard", 192–193
with children, 188–189
compliments, examples, 181–182
connection, maintaining, 214
date expenses, paying for, 183–184
date expenses, sharing, 184–186
Date Night Checklist, 60
Dating Kit contents, 179–182
do's and don'ts, 186–189
first dates, general, 191–192
intimacy, 194
mini-dates, suggestions for, 192–193
online dating, 217
perseverance, 198
preliminary considerations, 176
rebound dating, 20
thank you messages, examples, 196, 197
thank you messages, timing of, 197
wine choices, 134
wine tastings, 132
Dating Kit
contents, 179–182
defined, 256

Deglazing (cooking), defined, 256
Dice (cooking), defined, 256
Divorce
attorneys needed, 14
bucket list, 21
children, 17
children, effect upon, 18
cost factors, 15
general comments, 9
inventory worksheet, 16i
legal issues, 14
mediators, 11, 12
property inventory, 15
rebound dating, 20
recovering from, 19
Divorce Mediators
vs. Attorneys, 13
benefits of using, 12, 13
cost factors, 12
Do's and Don'ts
accessories, pillows and rugs, 75
candles, 73–75
dating, 186–188
dating and children, 188–189
decor, pictures and wall hangings, 72–73
flowers and plants, 75
living space, 71–75
online dating, background information, 227–229
online dating, profile photo, 221–225
wine, storing, 141

Downloads
    Date Night Checklist, 60
    Home furnishings list, 39
    Housekeeper cost/benefit analysis spreadsheet, 60
    Inventory Worksheet, 17

E
eBay.com, BBB coupons, 33
Ewing-Mulligan, Mary, *Wine for Dummies*, 145

F
First Big Date, defined, 257
Flowers and plants
    in bedroom, 78
    caring for, 76–78
    do's and don'ts, 75
    flowers vs. plants, 77
    low-light friendly, 78
    recommendations, 78
Fond (cooking), defined, 257
Francesconi, Marco, "How Humans Cognitively Manage an Abundance of Mate Options", 148
Frost, Robert, about dancing, 152

G
"George's Ten-Minute Rule"
    defined, 257
    meeting women, and, 171
girl+friend
    defined, 41, 257
    flower and plant advice, 78
    living space decor advice, 71
Good Knight, defined, 257
Good Knight pointer
    See also Chivalry
    anticipating your date's needs, 205
    anticipating your date's wishes, 74, 202
    BBB coupons, sharing, 34
    cell phones, silencing, 183
    dating, garage and yard sales, 212
    defined, 6
    dessert portion size, 104
    flowers, 76
    saying "thank you", 195
    wine knowledge, 128
"Grocery Cart Effect", defined, 84, 257

H
Happiness
    accumulation as substitute for, 26
    finding, 20
    life goal, 19
Helpful quotations
    appearance (Mae West), 165
    attitude (Winston Churchill), 227
    beer (Dave Barry), 200
    chemistry (Ron White), 173
    dancing (Robert Frost), 152

Index

de-cluttering and downsizing (George Carlin), 27
self-concept (Oscar Wilde), 230
"stacking the deck" (Jonathan Swift), 156
trust (Ernest Hemingway), 246
wine (Samuel Johnson), 145
Hemingway, Ernest, about trust, 246
Home. *See* Living space
Housekeepers and maids
  finding and hiring, 61–62
  Housekeeper cost/benefit analysis spreadsheet, 59
  housekeeping cost/benefits, 57–58
  Inverse Cleaning Theory of Hotness, 60–62
"How Humans Cognitively Manage an Abundance of Mate Options" (Lenton and Francesconi), 148
"How Much is Enough?" (Böll), 26
"How Much Will My Divorce Cost?" (Meyer), 15

I
Inverse Cleaning Theory of Hotness
  chart, 61i
  defined, 60–62, 258

J
Johnson, Samuel, about wine, 145

K
KISS (Keep It Simple, Stupid)
  complimenting, 167
  conversation, engaging in, 173
  defined, 258
  meeting women, 158

L
Lawyers. *See* Attorneys
Lenton, Allison P., "How Humans Cognitively Manage an Abundance of Mate Options", 148
Lichine, Alexis, about wine, 131
Living space
  ambiance, 71
  Date Night Checklist, 60
  de-cluttering and downsizing, 25–27
  do's and don'ts, 71–75
  furnishing, 29
  furnishing, list for, 39–40
  girl+friend advice, 71
  housekeepers and maids, 57, 58–59
  housekeepers and maids, hiring, 60–62
  housekeeping, 56
  housekeeping cost/benefits, 57i, 57–58

kitchen, basic setup, 87
laundry and dry cleaning, 62–63
planning, 22
renting, 23
requirements, 22
safety equipment, 36–37

M

McCarthy, Ed, *Wine for Dummies*, 145
Mean shifts, defined, 258
Meeting women
  appearance, 159
  approaching, 166, 170–171
  "Call the ball," 157–158, 167
  chemistry, 172
  classes, cooking, 83
  classes, dance, 152
  classes, group fitness, 150–151
  classes, Pilates and Yoga, 151
  compliments, examples, 168, 169
  conversation, engaging in, 35, 150, 156, 158, 168, 169
  conversation, integrating passion, 169–170
  creating first impressions, basic elements, 158, 173
  curiosity, inspiring, 170–172
  "George's Ten-Minute Rule", 171
  "Grocery Cart Effect", 84
  online dating web sites, 217
  professional organizations, joining, 153–154
  rejection, handling, 172
  shopping, Bath & Body Works, 155
  shopping, BBB (Bed Bath & Beyond), 34
  shopping, garage and yard sales, 35
  shopping, grocery stores, 84, 149–150
  shopping, shoe stores, 162
  shopping, Target stores, 178
  shopping, women's stores, 155
  taking continuing education classes, 154
  teaching continuing education classes, 154–155
  telephone number, asking for, 171
  volunteering, community organizations, 151–152
Meyer, Cathy, "How Much Will My Divorce Cost?", 15
Mince (cooking), defined, 258

Mini-Date
 defined, 258
 suggestions for, 192–193
Mise en place
 in cooking, 85
 defined, 258

O

Online dating
 See also Dating;
  Technology
 background, creating,
  230–232
 background, sample,
  232–234
 catching her eye, 235, 237
 chemistry, absence of,
  250–251
 details, keeping track of,
  249–250
 do's and don'ts, 227–229
 email, body, 235
 email, ending question,
  235, 239
 email, sample, 238,
  240–241
 email, subject line, 235,
  236
 Email inbox for a typical
  woman on a dating web-
  site, 236i
 email introductions, 234
 genuine interest, demon-
  strating, 238
 "Golden Rule", 251

"Golden Rule," defined,
 248
internal compass, 248
meeting women, strategies,
 218
multiple dating, 247–248
multiple dating, benefits,
 247–248
multiple dating, down-
 sides, 248–250
Orange Peel
 Consideration, 245–246
personal information,
 protecting, 244–245
pitfalls and scams, 244
profile, elements of, 219
profile, importance of,
 219–220
profile, upbeat and
 positive, 227
profile background,
 225–227
profile photo, 220
profile photo, bad
 example, 223i, 224i
profile photo, good
 example, 224i
saying "no thank you,"
 251
serial dating, benefits,
 246–247
serial dating, downsides,
 247
serial dating vs. multiple
 dating, 246–248
"winking", 234

Orange Peel Consideration
  defined, 259
  discussed, 245-246
  determining trust and subjectivity, 246

P
"Paparazzi Test"
  appearance, 160
  defined, 259
Primary photo, defined, 259
Products, cleaning
  Bar Keepers Friend, 67, 67i
  Cobra E-Z Plunger, 70, 70i
  general comments, 63–64
  Goo Gone, 68, 68i
  Magic Jetz Scrubz, 68, 69i
  Mr. Clean Magic Eraser, 69, 69i
  recommended products, 65–70
Products, home
  BD Rapid Flex digital thermometers, 43–44, 44i
  Bormioli Rocco Quattor Stagioni dipping bowls, 85–86, 86i
  candles, 74–75
  CDN ProAccurate Quick-Read Thermometer, 110, 110i
  cleaning products, general, 65–67
  Cuisinart Multiclad Pro Stainless Steel 12-piece cookware set, 89–90, 90
  evaluating before purchasing, 30–31
  fire extinguishers, 37–38
  flowers and plants, 78
  Friction tie rack and scarf hanger, 51i, 51–52
  Honey-Can-Do laundry sorter, 52i, 52–53
  OXO Good Grips 10-Piece POP container set, 47–48, 48i
  OXO Good Grips salt and pepper grinder set, 100, 100i
  OXO Steel CorkPull wine opener, 142–143, 143i
  Progressive International soap dispenser, 50i, 50–51
  purchasing, 31
  reviews, 41–54
  Skil 7.2v Lithium-Ion cordless screwdriver and drill, 53i, 53–54
  Skylink Security System deluxe kit, 45, 45i
  smoke and CO detectors, 36
  space measurement tools, 23
  Tervis tumblers, 41i, 41–42
  Victorinox 8-piece knife block set, 46i, 46–47
  Victorinox Fibrox 7-Inch Santoku knife, 47i

Woodlore cedar shoe trees, 42i, 42–43
Zak Designs 6-piece dinner sets, 49, 49i
Zionsville Candle Company soy candles, 75
Products, personal care
   Colgate Wisp mini-toothbrush, 180, 180i
   ear and nose hair trimmers, 165
   Philips Norelco Professional Body Grooming System, 164, 164i
Professional organizations
   finding, 153
   meeting women, 153
   Toastmasters International, 154
Profile, defined, 259

R
Recipes
   Creamy Fruit Dip (AKA Foolproof Dessert), 125–126
   Easy Peasy Hard Boiled Eggs, 119–120
   Fire-and-Forget Slow Cooker Chicken BBQ, 108
   Idahoan Mashed Potatoes, 118
   Mini Graham Cracker Jell-O Pudding Pie, 123–124
   online sources for, 82
   Sweet and Spicy BBQ Sauce, 106–107
   Toasted Baguette Slices, 121–122
   Winner, Winner Creamy Chicken Dinner, 109–110
   Wonderfully Fresh Chicken Caesar Salad, 111–113
   Zesty Short Ribs, 114–117
Relationships, starting
   See also Meeting women, Online dating
   long-term relationships, 184–185
   preparation for, 10–11, 55
   rebound dating, 20

S
Sauté (cooking), defined, 259
Sear (cooking), defined, 259–260
Secondary photos, defined, 260
Self awareness
   confidence, projecting, 166
   confidence-building techniques, 166–167
   first impressions, importance of, 158
   genuineness, 182
   internal compass, 19–20, 215
   as viewed by others, 148

Shopping
  being frugal, 34
  DSW Shoes, 162
  footwear and shoes, 161–162
  wine, 140
  Zappos (shoes), 161
Single Effort, defined, 260
Single Effort pointer
  children, involving, 24–25
  dating, brewery tours, 200
  dating, community education classes, 212–213
  dating, donating blood, 213
  dating, group fitness classes, 210
  dating, outdoor activities, 204
  dating, "photo walk", 201
  dating, planting trees, 208
  dating, progressive dinners, 211
  dating, visiting nursing homes and senior citizens' centers, 209
  dating, volunteering, 202
  dating, walking the dog, 203
  dating, wine tastings, 132
  defined, 5
  girl+friend advice, living space, 72
  meeting women, community education classes, 154–155
  meeting women, cooking classes, 83
  meeting women, dance classes, 152
  meeting women, garage and yard sales, 35
  meeting women, grocery stores, 84, 149–150
  meeting women, group fitness classes, 150–151
  meeting women, joining an organization, 153–154
  meeting women, shoe stores, 162
  meeting women, strategies for, 149–156
  meeting women, volunteering, 151–152
  meeting women, women's stores, 155–156
Sitting Idle at Step 2, defined, 260
So long! So what? Move on., defined, 260
Squashed grapes, defined, 260
Swift, Jonathan, "stacking the deck", 156

T
Technology
  See also Online dating
  cell phones, silencing, 183
  connection, maintaining, 214
  dating, online, 217

email messages, 214
message frequency, 215
personal information,
 protecting, 244–245
telephone call vs.
 email/text message,
 195–196
text messages, 214–215

U
Unray wayaay uicklyqay,
 defined, 260

W
Web sites
 allrecipes.com (recipes),
  82
 amazon.com (home
  furnishings), 31
 americastestkitchen.com
  (cooking), 82
 bd.com (thermometers),
  44
 boromiolaroccousa.com
  (dipping bowls), 86
 bucketlist.org, 22
 cdnw.com (cooking
  thermometers), 110
 colgatepalmolive.com
  (mini-toothbrush), 180
 consumerreports.org
  (product ratings), 37,
  110
 cookingforengineers.com
  (recipes), 116
 cooksillustrated.com
  (cooking), 82
 craigslist.org (housekeepers), 62
 craigslist.org (used
  furnishings), 34
 cuisinart.com (cookware),
  90
 decanter.com (wines), 140
 dsw.com (footwear and
  shoes), 162
 eBay.com (BBB coupons),
  33
 eharmony.com (online dating), 217
 en.wikipedia.org/wiki/Category:Professional_associations (professional organizations), 153
 epicurious.com (recipes),
  105
 foodnetwork.com (cooking), 82
 honeycando.com (laundry
  sorters), 52
 ikea.com (furniture), 53
 match.com (online dating), 217
 oxo.com (kitchen tools
  and utensils), 48, 100,
  143
 plentyoffish.com (online
  dating), 217
 progressiveintl.com (soap
  dispensers), 50
 richardshomewares.com
  (tie racks), 51
 SingleEffort.com/free, 17,
  39, 59, 60

skiltools.com (screwdrivers, cordless), 53
skylinkhome.com (alarm systems), 45
swissarmy.com (cutlery and knives), 46, 47
tervis.com (drinkware), 41
traderjoes.com (wine), 140
winespectator.com (wines), 140
woodlore.com (shoe trees), 42
zak.com (dinnerware), 49
zappos.com (footwear and shoes), 161
zionsvillecandlecompany.com (soy candles), 75
West, Mae, about appearance, 165
White, Ron, about chemistry, 173
Wilde, Oscar, about self-concept, 230
Wine
  basic facts, 129–130
  books about, 145
  Cabernet Sauvignon (red), 133–134
  Champagne, 135
  Chardonnay (white), 137–139
  Charles Shaw brand, 140
  chart, Wine pairing examples for common food categories, 144
  color, determination of, 131
  cooking, use in, 116–117
  cost of, 140
  cultural significance, 127
  defined, 260–261
  do's and don'ts, 141
  dry vs. sweet, 138
  films and movies about, 134
  grapes, types of, 129, 133i, 135i, 136i, 137i, 138i, 139i
  information sources, 140
  pairing with food, 137, 139, 143–145
  Pinot Noir (red), 134–135
  popular types reviewed, 132–139
  red vs. white, 130–131
  Riesling (white), 139
  Sauvignon Blanc (white), 136–137
  serving, 142
  shopping for, 140
  storing, 140–141
  tannin, 133
  variability of flavor, 129–130
  Zinfandel (red), 136
Wine for Dummies (McCarthy and Ewing-Mulligan), 145
Wink or winking, defined, 261

Worksheets and forms
    Date Night Checklist, 60
    Home furnishings list, 60
    Housekeeper cost/benefit
        analysis spreadsheet, 59
    Inventory worksheet, 16i

About the Author

Joe Keller is a father of two, an entrepreneur at heart, and a lifelong learner. His personal quest is to live a fulfilling, awesomely happy life and to help others do the same.

Single Effort grew out of Joe's learning curve following a painful divorce. Through trial and a healthy dose of error, Joe learned to approach single life – and life in general – with smarts and heart, leading to newfound confidence and exciting new adventures.

Equally at home cooking a meal for his kids, crooning karaoke on a night on the town, deciphering the world of dating for his readers, or traveling the globe, Joe believes that it's what's inside that counts – that happiness comes from following your passion, loving and being loved, and ultimately, finding peace within yourself.

Joe shares his passion for helping others through volunteer work in the U.S. and abroad, via his writing, and through public speaking. Joe makes his home in Auburn Hills, Michigan.

Learn more about Joe at **www.SingleEffort.com**.